Greetings from the Arrowhead

A Postcard Perspective of Historic Northeastern Minnesota

W9-BEV-374

Volume 1

THE NORTH SHORE & CANOE COUNTRY

TONY DIERCKINS

DULUTH, MINNESOTA

X-communication
The Carnegie Library
101 West Second Street, Suite 204
Duluth, Minnesota 55802
218-310-6541 • www.x-communication.org

Greetings from the Arrowhead, volume 1: a postcard perspective of historic northeastern Minnesota

Copyright © 2007 by Tony Dierckins

All rights reserved. No part of this book may be reproduced or transmitted
in any form by any means without written permission from the publisher.

Text, research, cover design, and interior design and layout by Tony Dierckins.
Further research by Maryanne Norton and Karin Gelschus.
Copyediting and editorial guidance by Scott Pearson.
Proofreading by Kerry Elliott and Suzanne Rauvola.

A complete list of image credits appears on page 103.

First Edition, 2007
07 08 09 10 11 • 5 4 3 2 1

Library of Congress Control Number: 2006939622
ISBNs: 1-887317-31-7; 978-1-887317-31-3

Printed in Singapore by Tien Wah Press.

Contents

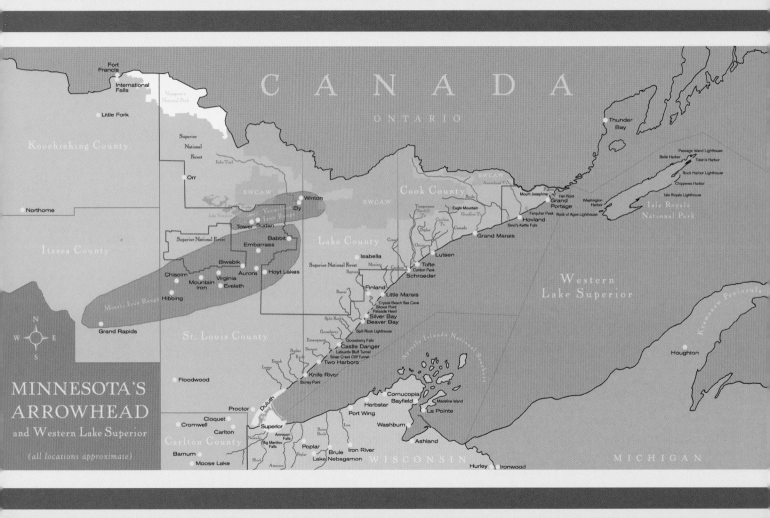

Greetings from Northeastern Minnesota!

As its subtitle implies, this book presents a "postcard perspective" of the Arrowhead region's history: a snapshot, a detail, a taste of which hopefully whets your appetite for more. If you finish this book and crave more Arrowhead history, I urge you to check out some of the fine titles listed in the References section.

The scope of this book follows the region's history through roughly the 1940s. The main reason we stopped at this point is because it marks the time when the lithographic postcard gave way to the modern "chrome" postcards—the same style of cards you can purchase today. (For an explanation on the history of lithographic postcards, see page vii.)

Not everyone shares the same perspective of the Minnesota Arrowhead region's geographic boundaries, but this book includes the counties most agree make up the region: Cook, Lake, St. Louis, Carlton, Itasca, and Koochiching (some say it should also include Aitkin, as that county contains the Cuyuna Iron Range; the novelty card on this page, which stretches the Arrowhead as far west as Bemidji, is based on a 1930s Work Projects Administration map designed to promote tourism). We've also included Isle Royale, which is actually a national park that belongs to the state of Michigan. But since most people visit-

A novelty postcard made as early as 1930 and no later than 1950 that stretches a little too far west of what most people consider the Arrowhead region, although it does make a clear case for the region's name. The map on the facing page provides a much more accurate view.

ing the island reach its shores on boats that depart from Grand Marais and Grand Portage, it is an essential part of the North Shore experience, and we've found room for it on these pages.

In case you were wondering, the second volume of *Greetings from the Arrowhead* will focus on the Iron Range, from mining towns such as Virginia and Hibbing (and many more) to Lake

Vermilion, the history of iron mining in the region, Voyageurs National Park, and more. Look for it down the road.

Readers who have picked up *Zenith: A Postcard Perspective of Historic Duluth*, may well recognize a few of the cards and some of the information presented in this volume. That's because this book also acts as a companion to and extension of *Zenith*, which contains a small section on the North Shore, Isle Royale, and the Superior National Forest. If you haven't seen *Zenith*, you may want to look it over; it includes a brief history of the Western Lake Superior Region that will help you gain more perspective on the history presented in this volume. *Zenith* covers the history of Duluth, Superior, and points along the Minnesota and Wisconsin Lake Superior shores—including the industries that helped shape the region—through 475 vintage postcards and 20 early paintings and etchings.

The majority of the postcards were supplied by several generous collectors, including Herb Dillon, Tom Kasper, Brad E. Nelson, Bob Swanfeld, Jerry Paulson, and Jerry Pepper (with a few from the Ely-Winton Historical Society and the author's private collection). Thanks to these gentlemen and a few other deltiologists, X-communication now has over 1,400 historic color images of the Arrowhead and the western Lake Superior region, we assume the largest such collection ever assembled—and it continues to grow. (We're always looking for more, so if you have some vintage lithographic postcards of scenes from the Arrowhead or western Lake Superior region, please contact us!) Many people provided or gave us permission to use the non-postcard images in the book, and you'll find a complete list of them on page 103.

And just as it took more than one person to assemble all these cards, it also took more than my efforts to research their subjects. The lion's share of research assistance for this volume was provided by Maryanne Norton and Karin Gelschus. We also had help from Melissa Estlow, Laura Jacobs of the Lake Superior Maritime Collection, Pat Maus of the Northeast Minnesota Historical Center, Rachelle Maloney of the Lake County Historical Society, Margaret Sweet and David Kess of the Ely-Winton Historical Society, the reference staff of the Duluth and Two Harbors public libraries; Glenn Nyman took the time to tell us all about Burley's Cabins, the resort his grandparents built in Ely, and church secretery Muriel Swardstrom sat us down in a pew and told us all sorts of fascinating stories about Two Harbors' First Presbyterian Church. I would of course be remiss (and in a heap o' trouble) if I forgot to mention those who helped me hone the book's text, such as copyeditor/editorial guru Scott Pearson and proofreaders Kerry Elliott and Suzanne Rauvola; I thank them for making me appear to be a better writer than I am.

— Tony Dierckins, December 2006

A Brief Word About Lithographic Postcards

Postcards have been a convenient form of communication since roughly 1861, and the color lithographic postcard saw its heyday from the turn of the twentieth century until about 1920 and continued to be a popular form of correspondence until the 1950s. Postcards have evolved over that time, making it relatively simple to guess the era during which a postcard was printed. Dating the actual image is much more difficult: publishers rarely indicated the year of a card's publication, and even if they did it couldn't be taken for granted that the image was from that date, as many photos were made into postcards years after they were taken. And postage cancellation markings aren't much help either, as cards were often mailed years after they were printed. But you can get a good idea of when a card was printed by recognizing a few clues in the manufacture of postcards from various eras.

Pioneer Era (prior to 1898). Only the federal government was allowed to use the word "postcard" on the back of these cards; privately published cards had to use terms such as "souvenir card" or "correspondence card." The government pre-printed its cards with one-cent stamps featuring Thomas Jefferson or Ulysses S. Grant; private cards required a two-cent stamp. There are no such cards in this book.

Private Mailing Card Era (1898–December, 1901). This period began when the government granted private printers the right to print their own cards with the inscription "Private Mailing Card." You can recognize a PMC by the fact that its back is not divided into message and address sections. In fact, until 1907 senders could write only an address on the back of the postcard; messages appeared only on the front.

Undivided Back Era (December, 1901–March, 1907). Since earlier cards already used the undivided back, the significant change was that the government now allowed private printers to use "postcard" or "post card" (one or two words) on the cards. During this time postcard popularity exploded, with sales doubling almost every six months.

Divided Back Era (March 1, 1907–1915). Known as the golden age of postcards, these cards featured the format we still see today: an image on the front, with the left side of the back reserved for a message and the right side for the recipient's address. Most of the cards from this era were printed in Germany because its lithographic printing technology was by far the most advanced.

White Border Era (1915–1930). World War I ended the supply of cards from Germany, and U.S. and English printers began making cards with inferior printing techniques. To save ink, a white border was left around "view" cards, giving the era its name. At the same time the telephone became affordable to more people, decreasing the practical need for postcards. Postcard collecting as a hobby also declined rapidly. (This time also saw the advent of the "Real Photo" postcard, produced not by lithography but by rotary drum imprinters; there are no such cards in this book.)

Linen Era (1930–1955). New printing processes in America revived postcards by allowing them to be printed on paper containing high "rag" (cotton) content, which gave the cards a textured feel and also allowed the use of vibrant inks, making them the most colorful lithographic cards produced in America. As you will discover, most of the cards in this volume are from the Linen and White Border eras.

Photochrome Era (1939–today). Photochrome cards look like actual color photographs, and today's postcards are produced using essentially the same method. This book contains no photochrome cards.

With the advent of photochrome postcards, lithographic postcard publishers began to fade away, and most were gone or had converted to photochrome by 1945. A few hung on through the 1950s, and the subjects of many of these cards were limited to motels along tourist routes, such as those you'll find in the "Scenic Highway 61" portion of this book.

A Divided Back card, which allowed senders to write their message on the card's back. Made between 1907 and 1915, these cards were printed in Germany during the postcard's "Golden Age."

White Border cards were made in the U.S. and Britain from 1915 to 1930, but were inferior in quality to the German-made cards. The white border saved ink during wartime.

Linen cards were made from 1930 until roughly the mid 1950s and marked an improvement in the quality of American cards. Lithographic cards began losing popularity with the advent of the photochrome card.

Part I

Greetings from the North Shore

Lake Superior

Lake Superior took shape from the receding waters of what geologists now call Glacial Lake Duluth. At the end of the last Great Ice Age, roughly ten thousand years before postcards, runoff from melting glaciers filled huge gouges the glaciers had sliced on their frozen journey south, carving what would become the Great Lakes. Over a thousand years or so, Glacial Lake Duluth drained down to the level of Lake Superior as the glacial dam to the northeast melted away, creating the largest lake in the world (unless you count the Caspian Sea as a lake).

Today the lake measures 383 miles east to west and roughly 160 miles north to south—31,820 square miles in all. With a volume of three quadrillion gallons, Lake Superior is home to 10 percent of the planet's fresh water.

By the time the big lake took its present shape the giant mammals that once roamed the region—woolly mammoths and mastodons, giant camels and ground sloths, short-faced bears and saber-toothed cats, and the giant beaver—all had become extinct.

From the end of the Great Ice Age until about 5,000 B.C., the region's human population consisted of small bands of Paleo-Indian cultures. Those hunters gave way to Eastern Archaic peoples, who thrived in the Great Lakes area until about 1,000 B.C. This group developed into a variety of cultures,

SURF DURING STORM   S.336

LAKE SUPERIOR, GITCHEE GUMEE, FATHER OF WATERS, DURING A NORTHEASTER

132-D—Sun Rays on Lake Superior

Minnesota's Scenic North Shore

including the Old Copper peoples who mined for copper on Michigan's Upper Peninsula and Isle Royale and refined the stone-working methods of their predecessors. The Eastern Archaic peoples gave way to the Woodland cultures.

As the Woodland cultures died out, the area became populated with the Dakota, meaning "friend" or "alliance of friends." French explorer Jean Nicollet called the Dakota *Naudowasewug*, "the snake," which pluralized in French is *Nadouessioux*, from which the term "Sioux" derives. (Descendants of these people today prefer Dakota.) It is unknown if the Dakota migrated to the area or descended from the Woodland Indians or even from the Old Copper culture, but by the time folks like Nicollet showed up, they populated Minnesota's Arrowhead Region. The Dakota eventually found life at the western edge of Lake Superior too crowded for comfort, as the eastern mi-

WHITECAPS ROLLING TO SHORE ON LAKE SUPERIOR   3A-H858

Gichigami or Gitchee Gummee?

Appropriately enough, the Ojibwe call the big lake *Gichigami* or "big water." "Gitchee Gummee" comes from, among others, Gordon Lightfoot's "Wreck of the *Edmund Fitzgerald*." (We trust the Ojibwe spelling.) In his epic poem "Song of Hiawatha," Henry Wadsworth Longfellow tells the tale of Hiawatha, his mate Minnehaha, and his grandmother Nokomis (the daughter of the Moon) whose wigwam stood near the "shining big-sea-water." The poem closes with Hiawatha accepting a Christian missionary's message, then departing into the west never to return, as the postcard at right depicts. In truth, Hiawatha was Iriquois, not Ojibwe.

58: The Departure of Hiawatha into the Sunset, Minnesota Arrowhead Country.
By the Shining Big Water, Stood the Wigwam of Nokomis.

TWILIGHT ON LAKE

Those Fur-loving French

From about 1550 until 1850, dandies throughout Europe wouldn't consider stepping outdoors without donning felt hats made from beaver underfur. This fashion trend became so popular that by the end of the sixteenth century, trappers had hunted the beaver to extinction in western Europe and nearly wiped the animal out in Scandinavia and Russia as well. So Europeans, particularly the French, looked to the New World for fur. Explorers such as Jean Nicollet, Jacques Marquette, Louis Joliet, Pierre Esprit Radisson, Sieur des Groseilliers, and Daniel Greysolon Sieur du Lhut—along with Jesuit missionaries including Marquette, Claude Jean Allouez (who most likely made the 1671 map of "Lac Tracy" below), and Louis Hennepin—traveled with French soldiers and native guides throughout the Great Lakes area. They mapped the region (which they claimed as New France) and

opened trade with the various tribes they encountered. Well established at Sault Ste. Marie and La Pointe, the Ojibwe became natural trading partners with the French.

gration of the Ojibwe brought competition and conflict. The Ojibwe were the largest tribe of the Algonkian peoples, a language group that includes the Potawatomi, Cheyenne, Fox, and Cree. Europeans often called the Ojibwe "Chippewa," which may have occurred from a misunderstanding or mispronunciation. (Ojibwe today also call themselves "Anishanabe," the "real" or "genuine people," which derives from *Anishinaubag*.)

The Ojibwe separated into four major groups midway through the seventeenth century and began expanding further west. This westward movement encroached on Dakota territory, and the two great peoples soon found themselves uncomfortable neighbors and, eventually, bitter enemies. The Ojibwe would later replace the Dakota on Lake Superior's western shores and

MOONLIGHT

S-356

BY THE SHINING BIG SEA WATER, GITCHEE GUMEE,

most of Minnesota. Then the Europeans arrived, and that changed everything.

French fur traders and trappers (known as voyageurs), along with Jesuit missionaries, arrived near the end of the sixteenth century, looking to trap beavers (see page 4). Soon enough the English were competing with the French, which sparked the French and Indian War, ending with a British victory. The American Revolution would eventually push the British into Canada and the western expansion of the United States later brought the region south of Canada under American control. The native peoples that populated the region were forced onto reservations in the nineteenth century.

Today Lake Superior is considered part of Michigan, Wisconsin, Minnesota, and Ontario, Canada.

124-D Shoreline, Minnesota's Scenic North Shore Drive

131-D—Breakers along the Shore of Lake Superior

Minnesota's Scenic North Shore Drive

ICEBERG ON LAKE SUPERIOR

HIGHWAY No. 1, NORTH SHORE, LAKE SUPERIOR, NEAR TWO HARBORS. 107542

ON HIGHWAY NO. 1. NORTH SHORE. LAKE SUPERIOR NEAR BEAVER BAY

Highway 61 (Old Highway 1)

The stretch of highway along the Minnesota north shore of Lake Superior began in 1879 as a simple brushed trail used by sled-dog drivers like John Beargrease to deliver mail in the winter (during summer months, all transportation along the north shore was done on the water). By 1900 a rough stage road was somewhat complete, but only passable in the winter by horse-drawn sleigh. Between 1900 and 1920 local communities along the lake built their own stretches of the road. Only the link between Duluth and Two Harbors was graded adequately for safe motor traffic, and from there to the Canadian border the road was little more than a narrow path, with many sections of road wandering miles from the shore. (Remnants of some of those roads remain, indicated by "Old North Shore Road" signs.)

In 1921 Minnesota made plans for a trunk highway system that included Highway 1, which would run from Iowa to Canada. The 154-mile stretch from Duluth to the Canadian border was known as the North Shore Drive (later the North Shore Scenic Drive) and was designed to stay as close to Lake Superior's northern coast as nature would allow. The roadway was first fully paved in 1933. It later became part of U.S. High-

HIGHWAY No.1, NEAR LUTSEN, NORTH SHORE, LAKE SUPERIOR. 107553

RIDGE ON HIGHWAY No.1, AT BEAVER BAY, NORTH SHORE, LAKE SUPERIOR. 107539

way 61, which reaches from New Orleans to Minnesota's Pigeon River at the Canadian border. A 1941 advertisement for the North Shore Drive noted that the North Shore, America's "Summer Playground" and "Hay Fever Haven," had no snakes or poison ivy.

In 1924, just three years after Minnesota began its trunk highway system, a bridge was built to span the Stewart River. Bridge No. 3589, a reinforced concrete arch adorned with Classical Revival details, stretches nineteen feet across the river. Because Lake Superior's North Shore tributaries are particularly rocky wa-

terways, the North Shore was one of only a few regions in Minnesota provided with the funds to build concrete bridges in the highway system's early years. The Minnesota Highway Department boastfully declared the bridge "the most aesthetically accomplished statement...produced by the state highway program."

Highway 61, of course, became as famous as Route 66 after the release of Bob Dylan's 1965 album *Highway 61 Revisited*. But Dylan's title song (and the rest of the album) had little to do with the actual Highway 61. In the song, the road is not literal, but, perhaps, a place to get rid of a bunch of red, white, and blue shoestrings and some telephones that don't ring.

ELMGREN MOTOR COURT — 10 MILES FROM DOWNTOWN — DULUTH, MINN.

"Scenic 61"

From Duluth you can drive to Two Harbors quickly on the Highway 61 Expressway or you can take the slow road: Scenic 61, which hugs the lake for about twenty-two miles.

One of the more popular stops along Scenic 61 is Stoney Point, a stretch of rocky shoreline along a loop of road at milepost 15. Just one mile up lies the Buchanan Wayside, marking the spot of an abandoned town named for President James Buchanan. The town, laid out in 1856, was the seat of the land office for Northeastern Minnesota. After the office relocated, the settlement disappeared.

Many of Lake Superior's tributaries empty into the big lake along this stretch, including the French River at milepost 11, the Sucker River at milepost 13, and the Knife River at milepost 18. All three rivers are known as great places to cast a line, and the French is home to the French River Hatchery, which produces walleye, herring, splake, chinook salmon, and both rainbow and lake trout. The Ojibwe called it *Angwassagozibi* (Floodwood River); they named the *Namebinizibi* or Sucker River for the fish that gather there annually to spawn.

The mouth of the Knife River (*Mokomanizibi* or "Sharp Stones River" to the Ojibwe) is also the location of the village of Knife River, which was platted in 1899 to serve the Alger-Smith Lumber Company's railroad. Russ Kendall's father opened a smoked fish house there in 1924 after his truck broke

down, forcing him to sell his smoked fish from the side of the road (Russ still smokes his own fish). In Knife River you'll also find Emily's Deli, originally opened by Emily Erickson (who emigrated from Norway when she was 12) in 1929 in a building that was once a general store and post office.

Like much of the North Shore, the stretch along Scenic 61 is dotted with cabin resorts, motels, and restaurants—many of which have come and gone. The Fish Fry Lodge was found on the site which is now the McQuade Safe Harbor, and the Elmgren Motor Court was found just west of the Fish Fry (it is now the Gardenwood Motel). The Loneyville Motel (which apparently featured a miniature farm), was located in the township of Larsmont, a few miles west of Two Harbors. The community was formed during the 1880s to serve a large logging operation, but didn't receive its name—for Larsmo, Finland, from which most of its setters hailed—until 1914. By then fishing and farming had become its chief industries. The House of Sweden, found just west of Two Harbors, was built by Walt Grant in 1946 and only served food from his native Sweden. The restaurant added motel rooms in the 1960s, and Grant sold the place to Tony and Marge Radosevich in the early 1970s; they converted it into the Earthwood Inn, which still operates.

NORTH SHORE DRIVE, MINNESOTA ARROWHEAD COUNTRY

Silver Creek Cliff

For years Highway 61's most breathtaking moment was driving along the Silver Creek Cliff, formed by volcanic activity more than a million years ago. Before it became part of the trunk highway system in the 1920s, the road actually diverted inland several miles to avoid the cliff. When the trunk highway was built, workers dynamited a section of the cliff and used steam-powered bulldozers to clear the rock, which was then carried off by horse-drawn wagons. This allowed a narrow road to pass along the lake side of the cliff, forming a giant blind corner. Little more than a small barrier separated the road—and travelers—from a significant drop to the rocky shores below. If that wasn't dangerous enough, boulders freed by erosion would often tumble down the side of the creek and onto the roadway.

The excitement ended in 1994 after a tunnel begun in 1991 was finally completed. The initial plan to make passing the Silver Creek Cliff safer involved widening the roadway to keep vehicles further from the edge, but engineers estimated that would

105 Silver Creek Cliff and Lake Shore Drive along Lake Superior
Historical Plaque in Left Foreground Sheer Above Gitchee Gumee

have required the removal of 1.5 million cubic yards of rock. The tunnel required removing only 500,000 cubic yards, and it's a stunning piece of engineering: 1,300 feet of roadway with tile-covered walls and continuous lighting, plus entry façades that complement the rocky hillside. The tunnel has made the passage much safer for drivers, particularly for the thousands of tourists—most of them unfamiliar with the highway's twists and turns—who travel the road each year. Of course, there are many North Shore residents who feel the tunnel has stripped the roadway of some of its charms.

During the 1950s a family of billy goats set up home on the cliff after escaping from a nearby farm. They spent four years on the cliff, peacefully grazing for food until a bobcat killed the doe and a kid born earlier in the year. The local sheriff then shot the buck, thinking it the most humane thing to do.

Further up the road Lafayette Bluff Tunnel is the only other tunnel along Highway 61. The bluff is named for the steamer *Lafayette*, which went down along with the barge *Manila* (which it was towing) during the infamous storm of November 28, 1905 (see page 37). The crews of both vessels made it to shore safely.

SILVER CREEK CLIFF ON HIGHWAY No. 1, NEAR TWO HARBORS

SILVER CREEK CLIFF, LAKE SUPERIOR NORTH SHORE DRIVE, TWO HARBORS, NEAR DULUTH, MINN.—4

International Border

The Pigeon River (see page 52) acts as the international border between the United States and Canada. It is here that U.S. Highway 61 ends only to become Canada's King's Highway 61, stretching to its final destination, Thunder Bay, Ontario. The city of Thunder Bay was created in 1970 (the bay itself had been there for quite some time) when the towns of Fort William and Port Arthur merged. Fort William was once the hub of the Canadian fur trade, formed in 1803 by the Northwest Company. Port Arthur grew out of Prince Arthur's Landing and incorporated in 1884.

BRIDGE OVER PIGEON RIVER, INTERNATIONAL BOUNDARY, HIGHWAY No. 1

107550

The Pigeon River Bridge. Boundary between Canada and U.S.
Port Arthur, Fort William and Duluth Highway.

INTERNATIONAL BOUNDARY LINE HIGHWAY No. 1.

107540

The card at top, made sometime after 1917, shows the "Outlaw" bridge, financed by auto clubs in Duluth and Port Arthur/Fort William but not authorized by any U.S. or Canadian governing body. It opened August 18, 1917, and was replaced in 1934 (depicted in the card directly above); that bridge was replaced in 1964.

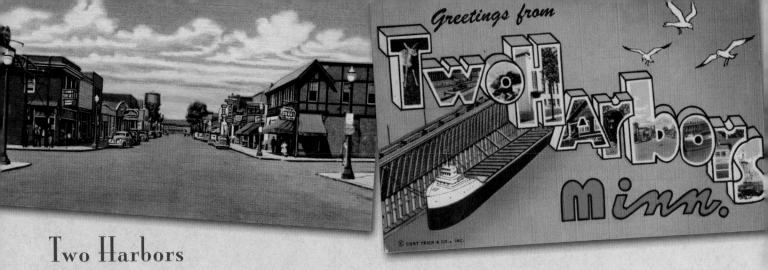

Two Harbors

Over the eons Lake Superior's waves carved two natural bays out of the northern coastline roughly twenty-two miles from Duluth. The Ojibwe called the site *Wasswewining*, "a place to spear by moonlight." In 1856 Thomas Saxon became the first European to settle at what would initially be named Agate Bay. The following year a sawmill sprang up in the adjacent bay, marking the birth of a settlement called Burlington. Outside of a little logging and some fishing, the two bays had no industry to support a population; the financial panic of 1857 also kept settlers away.

That all changed in 1884 when Charlemagne Tower's Duluth & Iron Range Railroad built an ore dock at Agate Bay to load ore transported from its Tower-Soudan mine on the newly opened Vermilion Iron Range.

The community boomed. One notorious two-block stretch on the southwestern edge of Agate Bay, "Whiskey Row," was the only land in town that was not owned by the D&IR and boasted twenty-two saloons in 1883; they all burned down two years later. Agate Bay and Burlington Bay came together in 1885, when the town of Two Harbors was officially platted. The town awarded its first liquor license four years later, but did not form a police department until 1907. Two Harbors, home to some of the world's largest ore docks, would grow to be the busiest port on Lake Superior outside of the Twin Ports (see page 28).

Lake County Courthouse

In 1888, four years after the Duluth & Iron Range Railroad Company turned Agate Bay into an iron ore port, the Lake County seat moved there from Beaver Bay. A two-story Queen Anne courthouse was built and served the county until 1904, when it was consumed by fire. Two years later architect James Allen MacLoed's Beaux Arts Courthouse—built of brick and stone and topped with a fish-scale-patterned dome—stood complete at 601 Third Avenue. The open dome sat over the courtroom, but it caused acoustic problems and was closed off in 1945.

Artist Axel E. Soderberg of Odin J. Oyen, a Lacrosse, Wisconsin, decorating firm, was called in a year after the building was complete to create a mural of "Law & Justice." He also executed three other murals representing commerce, mining, and forestry. Major restoration projects in the late 1990s and 2002 brought the building back to its original grandeur, even uncovering skylights long hidden by suspended ceilings.

Lake County Court House, Two Harbors, Minn.

Court House, Two Harbors, Minn.

Presbyterian Church

Found just across the street from the Lake County Courthouse at 531 Third Avenue, Two Harbors' First Presbyterian Church has stood since 1906. The original 1887 church (pastored by the Reverend J. N. Johnstone) was a simple frame structure, but its congregation's rapid growth made the building obsolete by 1900.

Church leaders, including the pastor, Reverend J. A. McGaughey, called on Duluth architects Fredrick German and A. Werner Lignel to design a building in the English Gothic style. Two Harbors contractors Gustafson and Strom constructed the building using red brownstone quarried near Port Wing, Wisconsin, and brought to Two Harbors on barges from Lake Superior's south shore. The building included a parapeted corner tower with a pyramid roof (seen in the postcard at right); that roof, unfortunately, is no longer part of the structure.

Inside the church, a slanted floor and curved wooden pews provide parishioners a theatre-like view of the altar. All but one of the building's stained-glass windows commemorate early parishioners; a lone panel was donated by local sailors in honor of thirty-three men who lost their lives during the storm

Presbyterian Church and Court House, Two Harbors, Minn.

of November 28, 1905 (see page 37). The church once had a pipe organ that, story has it, only worked when the furnace was in operation.

Over the years the church joined with Two Harbors' First Methodist Episcopal Church, the Swedish Methodist Episcopal Church, and the Clover Valley Presbyterian Church. In 1969 it joined with the Methodist Church and became the United Church of Two Harbors.

Central High School

While Two Harbors didn't have a high school until 1902, the Lake County School District (which included some of what is now St. Louis County) was organized in 1859, just one year after Minnesota became a state. It was managed by Gustav Weiland and had only one teacher, Jennie Clark. Agate Bay didn't have a schoolhouse until 1883, when $270 was spent on a log structure on a lot that later became the site of the D&IR roundhouse; a "Mrs. Stonehouse" was the teacher.

The need for schools grew after the passing of legislation in 1885 making it mandatory for children aged six to sixteen to attend school at least three months a year. Interestingly, many of the students were actually twenty-one years old or older, and most of the teachers themselves did not have a high school diploma.

By 1901, a high school was needed, and on February 12, 1902, a new $3,500 building was up at Fourth Avenue and Fifth Street. The school's three teachers educated fifty students on the topics of arithmetic, grammar, and American history. That year Mary Rylander and Ann Paulson became the school's first graduates.

Enrollment rose, and teachers and subjects were added. By 1910 the school's nearly one hundred students were learning

Central High School, Two Harbors, Minn.

music, Latin, sewing, and "scientifics" from seven teachers. There was also a course in "domestic services," and students could participate in athletics (the school had both a football and hockey team), the Debate Team, the Glee Club, and the Foreign Language Club. Twelve students, nine women and three men, graduated that year.

101:—LAKE COUNTY HIGH SCHOOL, TWO HARBORS, MINN.

47756

Two Harbors High School

By 1935 the students and faculty had outgrown the old Central High School building, and plans were announced for a new structure east of the existing structure.

Built by the Public Works Administation, the new building was designed in what some call Classical Moderne (or "PWA Moderne" in the U.S.), a subclass of the Art Deco movement. The Art Deco style is demonstrated the school's buff-colored brick, parapet trim of a decorative zigzag design, and glass block used in the entry tower. Inside the building's auditorium, Charles Morgan, Leroy Turner, and E. Holm painted murals. The building was estimated to cost about $100,000, but when the last brick was set in 1940, that price had risen to $585,000.

The building was constructed in phases, with the first portion completed in 1935. In 1939 a wing was added to the building's west side. The old high school was demolished that same year, replaced by a new building that brought the two wings together. A small part of the original high school remained: the smoke stack and coal bin were retained for the new structures. Later additions added more facilities to the complex, including a gymnasium (1954), a kitchen and swimming pool (1961), and a counselor's office (1964).

In the spring of 2004 the school was closed and the following September the new high school opened in a different location. The 1935 building could no longer be used because of physical and systemic problems beyond reasonable repair. The building still stands.

Dr. Budd's Hospital

Doctor J. Danley Budd had a long career before opening his hospital in Two Harbors. A native of Grant County, Wisconsin, Budd was educated at Lawrence University and went into the drug business before deciding to study medicine in St. Paul at the St. Paul Medical College (which later became part of the University of Minnesota). He spent eleven years practicing medicine in Michigan—six as an assistant surgeon for an iron company and five as a lumber company's physician.

Budd moved to Two Harbors in 1888 as the chief physician for the D&IR and established his hospital in 1896 in a two-and-a-half story wood-frame building on the corner of First Avenue and Maple Street, boasting accomodations for twenty-five patients (it later expanded to hold fifty), and the Budd family as well. In order to provide good lighting and sanitation, the entire operating theater was finished in white tile. The hospital had all the modern equipment available at the time, including an X-ray machine. Most of the hospital's early cases involved injuries that occurred in lumber camps and sawmills, at the ore docks, and on the railroad.

Dr. Budd was also one of the five founders of what would become 3M (see page 42), represented the region in at least one session of the Minnesota State Legislature, and was Lake County's Medical Examiner and Coroner. He also owned what was considered "probably the finest collection [of books] in the Northwest"—some two thousand volumes, over half of which featured elegant bindings or were rare editions.

The hospital is now the Lakeside Boarding and Lodging Home.

DR. BUDD'S HOSPITAL, TWO HARBORS, MINN.

Y.M.C.A. Building

The D&IR contributed greatly to the development of Two Harbors. In 1883 it built the Lakeview Hotel to serve as a boarding house for its employees. As ore production grew, the railroad grew as well, and its transient workers needed something to do with their time off. So the railroad found itself almost singlehandedly supporting the local Y.M.C.A., going as far as building it a clubhouse in 1898.

The structure, located at First Avenue and Seventh Street, was a large three-story wood-frame building that held an office, a "boy's room," a reading room, a parlor, a game room, a reception room, forty-eight sleeping rooms, and, as the *Duluth News-Tribune* reported, "well kept toilets with laundry." The facility also boasted a swimming pool, a gymnasium, and two bowling alleys.

Two years after it opened it had 400 members. Some of them organized a camera club and captured what were considered some of the "finest views in this vicinity." The facility was also used for religious, social, and educational work. In the 1920s its 960 members each paid annual dues of $5; the D&IR also paid a "substantial sum" each month for maintenance and repairs.

The Duluth & Iron Range Railroad Company built and maintained the Two Harbors Y.M.C.A. building. The "Y" was inextricably linked to the railroad, and older publications often refer to it as the "D.I.R.Y.M.C.A." or the "R.Y.M.C.A." It was torn down in 1962.

In 1923 the Two Harbors Y.M.C.A. opened a camp thirty-five miles away at Lake George and shared it with the Salvation Army. Boys and girls each spent three weeks at the camp, and the Salvation Army used it for another week.

COMMERCIAL STATE BANK.
TWO HARBORS, MINN.

COMMERCIAL STATE BANK

Planned, built and equipped by
A. MOORMAN & CO.
St. Paul, Minn

Commercial State Bank

The oldest bank in Lake County, Two Harbors Commercial State Bank was established by Captain Joseph Sellwood and D. A. Burke in 1889 as Sellwood, Burke, and Company. Its board of directors included Dr. J. D. Budd (see page 18) and John Dwan, who founded 3M (see page 42). The private bank reorganized in 1908 to comply with state bank laws and changed its name the same year.

The bank, built at 613 First Avenue in 1915, was made as safe as the technology of the time would allow. Its steel-lined vault included an electronic burglar alarm system that was added in 1921. Unfortunately, the bank's marble pillars were hauled away during a remodeling project in 1962.

Captain Sellwood, the bank's president, lived in Duluth and built the Sellwood Building that still stands at 202 West Superior Street and three homes at Eighteenth Avenue East and Superior Street (one for himself and his wife and two as wedding presents for his daughters). Sellwood also owned the Brotherton Mine near Lake Sunday in Michigan's Gogebic Iron Range. He had first come to Michigan from his native Cornwall, England, to work in northern Michigan's copper mines.

The bank sold in 1999; it is now known as the Lake Bank and has an office in Silver Bay.

First State Bank

Two Harbors' First State Bank organized in 1902 in a simple frame building at 610 First Avenue (now the home of the Electric Shop and True Value Hardware). That first year the bank received just $29,000 in deposits and loaned out $25,000 of it.

The bank's owners built the Classical-Revival building at 622 First Avenue (seen in the postcard) in 1916. In 1925 a unique protection system was installed in the bank's vault: if would-be burglars attempted to blow the vault, poisonous mustard gas would be released to chase off the thieves. (More likely, it would have killed them: mustard gas is a chemical agent introduced into warfare by Germany during World War I—the Germans dispersed it as an aerosol in bursting shells. Actually a colorless liquid, mustard gas can blister skin, cause blindness, and if inhaled, cause pulmonary edema in the lungs.) Bank staff also installed a cylinder in the vault in 1928 so that if anyone was accidentally locked inside, food and water could be passed through until the safe could be opened.

A national charter in 1925 changed the bank's name to the First National Bank of Two Harbors, and it was sold in 1929 to the Northwest Bancorporation, which eventually developed into Norwest Banks, which in turn became part of Wells Fargo. Today the bank is a branch of Wells Fargo.

First State Bank, Two Harbors, Minn.

Commercial Hotel

Records aren't clear about when the Commercial Hotel was built, but it was most likely in the late 1880s or early 1890s. It was probably owned by the D&IR Railroad, as its manager, N. McPhee, was described as "one of the most competent and popular hotel men on the D&IR." Once the largest hotel in town (found at First Avenue and Sixth Street), the Commercial stood three stories high and held twenty-two rooms. It catered to businessmen and hunting and fishing parties, and its dining facilities could seat fifty. Fire destroyed it in 1918.

The Federal Writer's Project of the 1930s recorded aging lumberman Dell Chase of Cornell, Wisconsin. Mr. Chase, who worked the woods twenty miles northeast of Two Harbors for a man named McPherson, told this tale of the Commercial:

"Mr. McPherson bought four fine horses at a sales stable in Duluth. He chose me out of forty men to go to Duluth and bring them in. So back over the forty-one miles [to Duluth] I went all alone. I got a train out of Two Harbors at 11 P.M. Friday and arrived in Duluth at 12:30 the next morning, twenty long, hard hours. The next morning I started for camp; had dinner at Knife River and spent the night at Two Harbors. There I saw a horrible fight. I saw the most feared man in the state—'Kill-Dee' was his name. He picked a fight with a Mr. Roch of Chicago Bay. Kill-Dee was an outlaw, well known in that part of the country. In this case he had borrowed ten dollars from Roch about two hours before and came back to get more, and so the trouble started. I was standing at the end of the bar in the Commercial Hotel, sipping a cold glass of beer after my two long, hard days. Roch stalled off as long as possible and then the fight was on. Up and down and over and around the bar and Kill-Dee reaching for his guns which he finally got. Tried twice for the kill but failed each time. Roch, a very skillful man, got the gun. He knew it was now or never, so he finished the job with a bullet between the eyes of Kill-Dee. The first shot Roch fired went over the bar among the bottles, the second went through the floor and lodged near the hip of a girl on the second floor. The third got the villain right between the eyes."

Commercial Hotel,
Two Harbors, Minn.

PHOTO BY BERGREN.

Rustic Inn

In 1923 Alice and Iver Admundson opened a hamburger stand at the corner of Third Avenue and First Street (also known as Park Road), and it quickly became a Two Harbors institution with a reputation for serving the best food in town, endorsed by famed food critic Duncan Hines.

The versatility of the Rustic's facilities made it the place for everything from card parties to public meetings. In the 1920s, the Duluth Eskimos, one of the first teams in the National Football League, held training camp at the Rustic (the Eskimos eventually became the Washington Redskins).

The business was so successful that over the years several additions were made to the original building. Considered one of the first businesses on the North Shore to cater to tourism, the Rustic actually prospered during the Great Depression thanks in part to its role as host to Civilian Conservation Corps camp workers. The owners also took advantage of the North Shore's reputation as a respite for allergy sufferers in the days before antihistamines: the Amundsons built eleven "Hay Fever" cabins which they rented to those from farming communities seeking relief during the summer. This aspect of the business was so popular they had to hire about twenty high school students during their summer break.

The Rustic Inn closed in 1958, driven out by competition from drive-in fast food establishments; the land where it stood is now home to the Harbor Point Apartments. Another Rustic Inn was started just ten miles to the northeast in Castle Danger in the 1920s by a man named Edison, but has no connection to the Two Harbors establishment. The business is still open and the building retains its original logs.

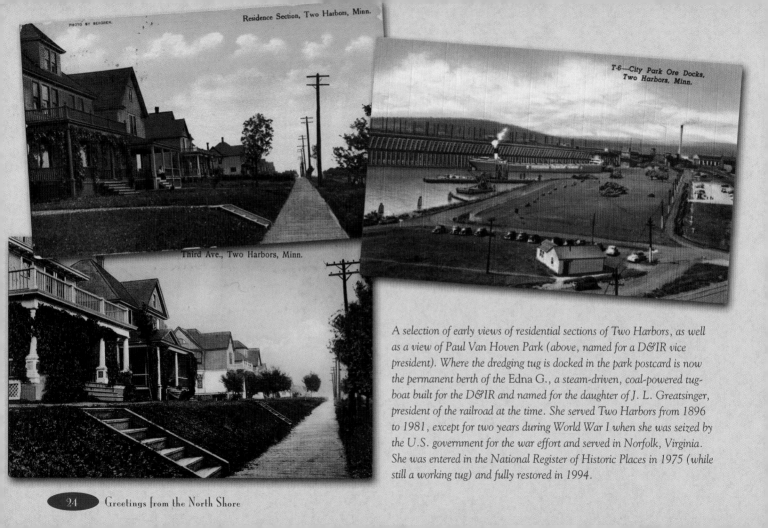

PHOTO BY BERGREN.

Residence Section, Two Harbors, Minn.

T-6—City Park Ore Docks, Two Harbors, Minn.

Third Ave., Two Harbors, Minn.

A selection of early views of residential sections of Two Harbors, as well as a view of Paul Van Hoven Park (above, named for a D&IR vice president). Where the dredging tug is docked in the park postcard is now the permanent berth of the Edna G., a steam-driven, coal-powered tug-boat built for the D&IR and named for the daughter of J. L. Greatsinger, president of the railroad at the time. She served Two Harbors from 1896 to 1981, except for two years during World War I when she was seized by the U.S. government for the war effort and served in Norfolk, Virginia. She was entered in the National Register of Historic Places in 1975 (while still a working tug) and fully restored in 1994.

Two Harbors Light Station

The advent of iron mining had turned Two Harbors into somewhat of a boomtown. Not only was the iron ore industry causing increased harbor traffic, but coal carriers, lumber vessels, various commercial boats, and passenger ships added to the congestion. Thirteen hundred ships passed through Agate Bay alone in 1892, just eight years after the first load of Vermilion Iron Range ore left its docks. Breakwaters were built to make the harbor safer, but it needed a lighthouse. In March 1891 the U.S. government paid Thomas Feigh one dollar for an acre of land and almost immediately began work on a lighthouse. The lighthouse's fourth-order Fresnel lens was lit for the first time on April 15, 1892.

The twelve-foot-square tower stands just shy of fifty feet in the air and includes a watch room, a lantern room, a cleaning room, and even an extra bedroom for a second assistant keeper.

The light tower connects to the keeper's house, allowing the keeper passage without going outside in the winter. The tower's walls are built in three layers of brick, the house's with two; where they meet the wall is five courses thick, engineered to act as a fire break to keep the keeper's family safe (the lamp oil was highly combustible).

The postcard above celebrates the North Shore's reputation for severe winter weather. The Two Harbors Light Station is shown in the lower-right panel. The image at left is a detail from the postcard.

Memorial Engine "Three Spot"

Two Harbors is home to the memorial engine Three Spot, a steam locomotive built by the Baldwin Locomotive Works of Philadelphia, Pennsylvania, and shipped to Duluth by rail in 1883. A scow and a tugboat then hauled it to Agate Bay, a predecessor of Two Harbors. There the Three Spot became the first engine of the Duluth & Iron Range Railroad. The locomotive pulled the first load of Vermilion Range iron ore sixty-eight miles from Soudan, Minnesota, to the brand-new D&IR dock on July 31, 1884.

The Three Spot was sold for scrap in 1920, but the D&IR's Thirty Year Veterans Club purchased the engine before it was destroyed and put it on display in 1923. It is currently on display with the Duluth, Missabe & Iron Range Railway's engine "229" at the depot in Two Harbors.

MEMORIAL ENGINE "3 SPOT," D. & I. R. R. R., NEAR DULUTH, MINN.—70
FIRST ENGINE BROUGHT TO TWO HARBORS ON A SCOW IN 1883

U.S.C.G. Cutter *Crawford*

The *Crawford* was a Coast Guard Active-class cutter built at the New York Shipbuilding Corporation's yards in Camden, New Jersey, in 1927. She served Two Harbors from the time of her launch until 1937, when she was transferred to Buffalo, New York. During World War II she was stationed in Philadelphia and San Juan, Puerto Rico, before being decommissioned in 1947. The cutter was named for William H. Crawford, Secretary of the Treasury under presidents James Madison and James Monroe.

TWO EXCURSION BOATS LANDING AT TWO HARBORS, MINN.

U. S. COAST GUARD CUTTER "CRAWFORD," TWO HARBORS, MINN.—52

The Steamer *America*

Like every other community along the North Shore and Isle Royale, Two Harbors was served by the steamer *America* (above, foreground). Owned by a subsidiary of the A. Booth Company, the *America* replaced the company's *Hiram R. Dixon* and was piloted first by Jacob F. "Fog King" Hector and later by Edward "Indian" Smith. She ran between Duluth and Port Arthur (Thunder Bay) three times a week, delivering mail, supplies, and people from 1902 to 1928. In 1902, $6 bought you a round-trip journey, complete with meals and a berth. For more about the *America*, see page 57.

ORE DOCKS, TWO HARBORS, NEAR DULUTH, M

Bird's Eye View of Two

Two Harbors' Ore Docks

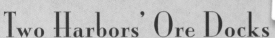

As you have most likely read by now, Charlemagne Tower's Duluth & Iron Range Railroad built an ore dock at Agate Bay (now Two Harbors) in 1883; a year later the dock accepted its first load of Vermilion Iron Range ore, ten cars full pulled from Soudan, Minnesota, by the steam locomotive Three Spot (see page 26). The railroad became the property of Illinois Steel in 1887, and in 1901 part of U.S. Steel; it was officially merged with U.S. Steel's Duluth, Missabe & Iron Range Railway in 1938. The railroads would eventually build six docks at Two Harbors.

Ore demand increased dramatically during World War II, and in 1944 the DM&IR docks in Duluth and Two Harbors broke loading records three times. The docks set a forty-eight-hour loading record by filling sixty ships with 649,275 tons of ore between Sunday, May 28, and Tuesday, May 30. And they didn't stop. The following day they broke the seventy-two-hour record when the loading total reached 859,959 tons. And from that Wednesday morning at 7 A.M. until the same time Thursday morning, crews loaded 406,484 tons, setting the single-day record in the process. (The previous twenty-four-hour record was set in 1942 with 337,180 tons.)

They reached an all-time high of 49 million tons in 1953. As the iron-rich ore was mined out, the docks slowed down. The Two Harbors docks actually closed from 1963 to 1966, when the mining industry picked up again with the development of taconite. Three docks remain, two of them still in operation.

T-5—Ore Docks, Two Harbors, Minn.

The three ore boats docked at the right in the card above are whalebacks,
built in Superior between 1888 and 1898 by their creator, Captain Alex-
ander McDougall, at his American Steel Barge Company. Often called
"pig boats" because of their appearance, whalebacks were the predecessors
to today's modern ore carriers, which implement many of the whaleback's
revolutionary ideas.

Scene along the Banks of the Stewart River, near Two Harbors, Minn.

STEWART RIVER, NEAR TWO HARBORS ON HIGHWAY No.1

NORTH SHORE OF LAKE SUPERIOR

107546

Stewart River

Located three miles northeast of Two Harbors, the Stewart River takes its name from early pioneer John Stewart, who settled in the area in 1856. Logging occurred along the Stewart in the nineteenth century, but the river was so rocky and narrow it often jammed with logs.

Today the mouth of the Stewart is a popular place to catch lake trout or to stop for a piece of pie at perhaps the North Shore's most famous eatery, Betty's Pies. Betty and Lloyd Lessard opened their shop in 1956; the original building—the former Andy's Fish Shack—was demolished in 1984, two years after Betty sold the enterprise.

ENCAMPMENT RIVER ON HIGHWAY No. 1

NORTH SHORE OF LAKE SUPERIOR   107547

Encampment River

In 1921 Thomas Winter described the Encampment River as "a beautiful trout stream cascading through a rocky gorge, leaping in several falls down the hillside, with here and there deep pools where the trout lie." Winter, along with Edwin Hewitt and Frances Shenehon, had just purchased 1,575 acres surrounding the Encampment from the estate of Two Harbors resident John Olson.

Doing so, they created the Encampment Forest Association and inadvertently helped preserve a small portion of Minnesota's original pine forest. Since it was private land throughout the peak of North Shore logging in the 1890s, the area was remarkably intact and makes up part of the remaining 1 percent of the state's pine forest. Today the area surrounding the river contains white pines that are over two hundred years old (white pines are susceptible to blister rust, a disease imported from Europe) and an abundance of ancient cedars.

The Encampment itself begins in a large swamp about twelve miles north of the lake shore. It winds its way south, dropping forty feet down its Upper Falls and, a half mile later, another twenty as it passes over Lower Falls (pictured in the postcard). Encampment Island is found offshore near the mouth of the river, just south of where the steamer *Lafayette* sank in the great storm of 1905 (see page 37).

Gooseberry River & Falls

The Gooseberry River appeared on explorers' maps as early as 1670. The river's name comes from the Ojibwe *Shabonimikanisibi* ("the place of gooseberries river"), although some say it was christened in honor of French explorer Sieur des Groseilliers, who explored the area in the 1660s with Pierre Esprit Radisson (*Groseilliers* is French for "currant bushes").

The river has an estuary at its mouth, which made it an ideal place for voyageurs to stop and camp.

The Nestor Logging Company set up camp at the river's mouth between 1900 and 1909, using two narrow-gauge rail lines to bring logs to the estuary, where the timber was tied into rafts and towed by tugs to mills in Baraga, Michigan, or Ashland, Wisconsin. One such raft contained six million feet of logs and took eight days to reach Baraga.

In the late 1920s the state of Minnesota bought 638 acres of land along the river from the estate of Wisconsin's Henry Vilas. It was intended to be a game preserve and pub-

136-D—Gooseberry Falls and River, Minnesota's Scenic North Shore Drive

87   GOOSEBERRY FALLS AND RIVER ABOVE U. S. HIGHWAY 61 BRIDGE, NORTH SHORE DRIV

GOOSEBERRY STATE PARK, MINNESOTA ARROWHEAD COUNTRY

lic hunting ground, but in 1934 it became a state park, and the Civil Conservation Corps went to work on it. From 1934 to 1941 the CCC built twenty-seven rustic structures made of stone and wood throughout the park, including administration buildings, officers' quarters, barracks, a mess hall, and a latrine. They also created picnic shelters and indoor facilities with kitchens, a sanitation building, and several picnic tables with surrounding fireplaces. Gooseberry's CCC unit included two Italian stone masons, John Berini and Joe Cattaneo, brought in to oversee and execute the intricate stone work still found in the park.

Today the park has been expanded to 1,687 acres and features three of the river's five waterfalls, including Upper Falls, which drops seventy-five feet, and Lower Falls, which cascades three hundred feet. In 1996 the park's facilities received a major makeover: a new bridge over Highway 61 and an award-winning Visitor's Center designed by Duluth architect David Salmela, which features a fireplace made from stone blasted out of the Silver Creek Cliff Tunnel. More than 570,000 people visit the park each year.

The linen card above, made between 1930 and 1950 and showing Gooseberry Falls State Park's Upper Falls on the Gooseberry River, is actually an oversized novelty card, which is why it has a nearly square shape. Cards of this size required extra postage to send through the mail.

LITTLE TWO HARBORS, NORTH SHORE, LAKE SUPERIOR.

107537

LITTLE TWO HARBORS AND SPLIT ROCK LIGHTHOUSE, NORTH SHORE, LAKE SUPERIOR ON HIGHWAY No. 1

Little Two Harbors & Other North Shore Fishing Villages

Little Two Harbors was once a Norwegian fishing camp kept by about fifteen herring fishermen who lived in tar-paper shacks. The tiny facility also allowed boats to bring supplies for the Split Rock Lighthouse keeper and his family. Only a few building foundations remain.

Commercial fishing on the North Shore first began in 1834, when the American Fur Company set up fisheries on Encampment Island, Grand Portage, and Isle Royale. In 1839 they caught five thousand barrels of fish, but there was no market for the high yield. By 1842, the company ceased operations.

The industry remained dormant until Scandinavian immigrants began arriving in the 1870s. Fisheries popped up in every settlement along the shore and Isle Royale, harvesting chubs, yellow perch, sturgeon, lake trout, and especially herring and whitefish by the ton. Outfits such as Duluth's A. Booth Company supported their fisherman by sending steamers, including the *America* (see pages 27 and 57), to supply the villages, allowing mostly Norwegian (with some Finnish and Swedish) fisherman to spend more time working the waters. Booth and other fisheries found markets for their yield in Minneapolis, St. Paul, Chicago, Kansas City, and St. Louis.

Herring fishing on the lake reached its peak in the early 1890s, providing 146 million pounds—78 percent of herring caught in the U.S. The industry reached its peak in 1915 with

DRYING NETS, FISHING VILLAGE ON HIGHWAY No. 1, NORTH SHORE LAKE SUPERIOR   2A-H313

Scenic North Shore Drive   2A-H244

The cards on this page show typical North Shore fishing villages, with nets hung on drying reels typically twelve feet long and five feet wide and made of cedar poles and pine. Before those made of nylon replaced them, cotton nets dried quickly and had to be removed immediately lest they "burn" in the sun. The nets were protected from corrosion with a bluestone treatment, which also removed accumulative slime.

11290.   Fishing Village, North Shore, Lake Superior.

a record catch of 20 million pounds in Duluth alone. In the 1920s, more than two hundred fisherman operated between Beaver Bay and Pigeon River alone. The 1930s were a different story. The lake's catch dwindled to below 8 million pounds. To survive the Great Depression, fishermen around Two Harbors organized the Icy Waters Fish Mart to market herring. The group sold herring fillets and smoked herring to Hormel and Walgreen's drugstores. The industry never quite recovered. Predatory lamprey eels and over-harvesting nearly wiped out the trout in the 1950s. Today the lake annually brings in less than two thousand pounds of fish.

Little Two Harbors & Other North Shore Fishing Villages   35

Split Rock Lighthouse

Split Rock Lighthouse, on Lake Superior's North Shore Drive, Minnesota Arrowhead Country

The Lake Superior storm of November 28, 1905, which damaged more than twenty-five ships and claimed thirty-three lives (see next page), also left two ships foundering on the rocky shoreline near the Split Rock River—then considered "the most dangerous piece of water in the world." Soon after, a local delegation went to Washington, D.C. to state its case, and in 1907 Congress appropriated $75,000 for a lighthouse and fog signal near the Split Rock.

Immigrant workers built Split Rock Lighthouse, a fifty-four-foot octagonal brick tower, between 1909 and 1910. The lens, a bivalve third-order Fresnel, was set in motion on July 31, 1910, after the lighthouse's first keeper, Orrin "Pete" Young, lit the incandescent oil vapor lamp for the first time. From its position high atop a North Shore cliff, the lighthouse's lens had a focal plane of 168 feet, the highest of all lights on the Great Lakes. By 1939 it was considered the most visited lighthouse in the U.S. and is still one of the North Shore's most popular tourist attractions.

The oversized linen card above was sold as part of a set with other oversized cards, such as the one of Gooseberry Falls on page 33.

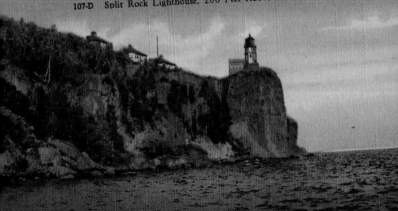

107-D Split Rock Lighthouse. 200 Feet Above Beautiful Lake Superior

The 1905 Storm: The Need for a Lighthouse

Twenty-five ships went down in Lake Superior during the storm of November 28, 1905, including the *Madeira* (pictured below), whose wreck helped plead the case for a lighthouse at Split Rock. The *Madeira* was under tow of the *William Edenborn*; the *Edenborn*'s captain cut the tow line thinking it would be safer for the *Madeira*. It wasn't. The ship struck Gold Rock, north of where Split Rock Lighthouse now stands. Crewman Fred Benson grabbed a coil of rope and climbed a sixty-foot cliff while the storm raged about him. He then dropped the rope to the *Madeira* and saved eight other crew members. Only the first mate perished, pulled down with the ship as he tried to climb the mizzenmast and jump to safety. The need for the lighthouse along that stretch of shoreline was bolstered by the wrecks of the *Lafayette* and *Manila* during the same storm.

John Beargrease

The most famous among the Ojibwe who lived in Beaver Bay was John Beargrease, born in Beaver Bay in 1858, the son of a minor Anishinabe chief named *Makwabimidem* (Beargrease).

Along with his brothers, John delivered mail along the North Shore from 1879 to 1899. During the summer he used a small boat he either sailed or rowed up and down the shore each week. In the winter months Beargrease used a dogsled on Lake Superior's ice whenever it was frozen enough to allow safe passage. At times the sled held nearly five hundred pounds of mail. Bells on the dogs, used to frighten away wolves, heralded the arrival of Beargrease (and the mail) to villages from Beaver Bay to Pigeon River. When the Old North Shore Road was complete in 1899, Beargrease lost his business to carriers using horse-drawn stages.

Beaver Bay is home to an Ojibwe cemetery, where Beargrease, his wife Louisa, and other members of his family lay in rest. Today the annual John Beargrease Sled Dog Race commemorates his efforts.

Beaver Bay

Beaver Bay is the oldest continuous European settlement along the North Shore, established in 1856 (two years after the Treaty of La Pointe allowed white settlement along the North Shore) by a group of ten families of German immigrants who moved to the area from Maumee, Ohio. The town was the seat of Lake County from 1866 until 1888, when the seat moved to Two Harbors. The community's first business was a sawmill set up by the four Weiland brothers (Frederick Wei-

BEAVER RIVER, NEAR TWO HARBORS, HIGHWAY No. 1, LAKE SUPERIOR

land was the first person of European descent born in Lake County). The Weilands' sawmill allowed the community to ride out the panic of 1857 and for twenty-five years it remained the town's main source of employment. The mill even hired some Ojibwe people, who came to the area to find work at the bay they called *Gajiikensikag*, "the place of little cedars." The Weilands later tried to bring an ore dock to Beaver Bay, but the D&IR chose to build theirs at Agate Bay, which later became Two Harbors.

Despite the lumber mill and local logging efforts, Beaver Bay's chief industry by 1910 was commercial fishing. Tourism has acted as a large part of the town's economy since 1924.

Beaver River, near Two Harbors, Minn.

SHORE LINE NEAR BEAVER BAY ON HIGHWAY No.1, NORTH SHORE, LAKE SUPERIOR.   107538

Palisade Head

135-D—Palisade Lookout at Castle Rock, Minnesota's Scenic North Shore Drive

Palisade Head, a cliff that climbs 348 feet above Lake Superior near the mouth of Palisade Creek, stands four miles up the shore from Silver Bay. (Silver Bay was created in 1954 by the Reserve Mining Company for workers at its taconite processing plant.) This eighty-acre precipice, formed by ancient volcanic activity, provides one of the most spectacular views of the lake and its shoreline. On clear days visitors can see the Apostle Islands, thirty miles away off Wisconsin's south shore, as well as the Sawtooth Mountains up along the shore (see sidebar) and nearby Shovel Point—sometimes called "Little Palisades"—which rises 180 feet above the big lake. Both Shovel Point and Palisade Head are part of Tettegouche State Park, which takes its name from the old Alger-Smith logging camp established in 1898 by eastern Canadians near Mic Mak Lake (named for an Algonquian Indian tribe from New Brunswick, Nova Scotia).

Today the sheer face of Palisade—igneous rhyolite overlaying soft basalt that has been undercut by Lake Superior's waves—provides perfect conditions for rock climbers who brave to ascend it.

Sawtooth Mountains

Actually lava deposits left behind by ancient volcanoes, the Sawtooth Mountains stretch nearly thirty miles between the Temperance River and Grand Marais. Colonel Charles Whittlesy named their highest point Carlton Peak in 1848 after climbing it with Rueben B. Carlton, for whom Carlton County is also named. Other high points in the "range" include Good Harbor Hill and Farquhar Peak.

Baptism River & Ilgen Falls

Called *Au Bapteme* by French voyageurs, the North Shore's Baptism River drops 700 feet before reaching Lake Superior, making it home to several waterfalls. The most spectacular of these is High Falls, a 70-foot drop—second only to the Pigeon River's 120-foot High Falls in all of Minnesota (see page 52)—located a mile or so from the entry to Tettegouche State Park. The river also contains Two-Step Falls, found downstream from High Falls. Though not as tall, Two-Step spills over some spectacular rock formations. Ilgen Falls (sometimes spelled "Illgin Falls" and misidentified in the postcard below as "Elgin Falls") is found upriver from High Falls and drops the river 35 feet where it roils into a cauldron on its way downstream. It takes its name form nearby Ilgen City, established in 1924 by Rudolph Ilgen and his family, who moved from Des Moines, Iowa, bought some land from 3M (see next page), and set up a sawmill, store, hotel, and cabins.

In 1910 the Alger-Smith Lumber Company sold its logged-out land surrounding the Baptism to the "Tettegouche Club," a group of Duluth businessmen, for use as a fishing retreat. The property was later sold to the deLaittres family, who acted as its stewards until the land became a state park in 1979. The park also adopted Baptism River State Park, which had been created in 1945.

145-D—Elgin Falls on Baptism River on Scenic North Shore Drive of Lake Superior

Crystal Beach Sea Cave

The Crystal Beach sea cave (called the "Cave of Waves" in the postcard below) is a pretty tricky place to get to, but it's well worth the time and trouble. Found near milepost 60 on Highway 61, the cave—more of an arch, really—is one of the largest on Lake Superior, carved from the rock by the lake's relentless waves. You can't get in the cave from the beach without a kayak or canoe, but you can see it fairly close up. It lies to the east of a horseshoe-shaped beach surrounded by cliffs where Crystal Creek empties into Lake Superior.

Ruins of abandoned structures indicate that this area was once the birthplace of Minnesota Mining and Manufacturing, better known today as 3M, one of the largest companies in the world. In 1902 Two Harbors attorney John Dwan and a few of his friends organized the company, intending to set up a mining operation along the shore at Crystal Bay near the Baptism River to extract corundum, an abrasive used in grinding wheels—it would have been one of only two such operations in North America. Unfortunately, the mineral they mined at Crystal Bay was not corundum but anorthosite, a much less valuable product. The company nearly collapsed before St. Paul's Lucius P. Ordway bailed them out. They set up a sandpaper factory in an old Duluth flour mill, but the inferiority of the anorthosite and Duluth's humidity almost crushed them again. Ordway then moved the company to St. Paul where it thrived—and continues to do so.

By the way, some folks from the Silver Bay area call this spot "Peterson's Beach," and it was once a popular spot to enjoy a fire and a few beers.

163-D—Cave of the Waves
Scenic North Shore of Lake Superior

151-D—Beautiful Falls on the Manitou River, Lake Superior
North Shore Drive

Manitou Falls, Lake Superior North Shore Drive

Manitou River & Falls

Named for the Ojibwe word for "spirit," the Manitou River is the heart and soul of Crosby-Manitou State Park. The park takes half its name from the river and the other half in honor of George H. Crosby, who in 1955 donated the 3,320 acres of land on which this park sits. Crosby owned and managed iron mines and helped develop the Mesabi and Cuyuna iron ranges. Officials decided the park should remain largely undeveloped, and so it only contains campsites for hikers—in fact, it was the first "backpack" park established in Minnesota and contains twenty-three miles of hiking trails. The falls pictured in the postcards drop more than sixty feet.

Caribou River & Falls

You won't find caribou anywhere near the Caribou River—they've been gone for more than one hundred years, ever since hunting, logging, and warmer temperatures destroyed both the animals and their habitat. You will, however, find one of the best waterfalls along the North Shore, especially during the spring thaw when the swollen river practically leaps off the cliffs.

The river and its falls are part of Caribou Falls State Park, which is little more than a parking lot, some outdoor toilets, and a hiking trail that leads to the falls and, eventually, to the Manitou River and Crosby-Manitou State Park, about six miles away.

According to legend, Edward Silver claimed 160 acres along the river—which was as yet unnamed—and his brother Henry made a similar claim on an adjacent piece of land. The Silvers chose the name "Caribou" for the river after Swamper Caribou, an Ojibwe trapper who worked the area each fall and winter and kept a home on its banks. The area developed into the township of Cramer, named for store owner Joseph Cramer.

Like many North Shore rivers, the land surrounding the Caribou was logged by the Alger-Smith Company, who created a nine-mile ice road along its banks. The year they cleared the Caribou River valley, it snowed so much that after one storm alone it took eighteen teams of horses to plow the road.

Cross River

Missionary Frederic R. Baraga, born in Yugoslavia in 1797, came to the United States in 1830 to devote his life to the American Indians of the Upper Great Lakes and was named Bishop of Upper Michigan in 1853 (Baraga, Michigan, is named for him). But before that, he had a little trouble in a canoe.

CROSS RIVER HIGHWAY No. 1

CROSS RIVER, NORTH SHORE DRIVE, BETWEEN TWO HARBORS AND GRAND MARAIS, NEAR DULUTH, MINN.—43

Crossing thirty miles of open Lake Superior waters from La Pointe on Madeline Island ten years prior to becoming a bishop, he and some Ojibwe guides encountered a storm that almost claimed their lives. They eventually found harbor at the mouth of a gently flowing river, and there Baraga nailed a wooden cross to a stump and wrote upon it, "In commemoration of the goodness of almighty God in granting to the Reverend F. R. Baraga safe passage from La Pointe to this place, August, 1843." The river became Cross River, and the wooden cross has since been replaced by one made of concrete.

The Ojibwe call the river the *Tchibaiatigozibi* or "Wood of the Soul River." It flows through the town of Schroeder, named for a logging company president whose firm harvested white pine along the river's banks around 1900. Two saloons and a bordello served the lumberjacks, keeping them—and their money—from heading for Duluth on their days off. In the 1880s (long before the logging company came) fisherman Henry Redmyer and his family set up a homestead on the river.

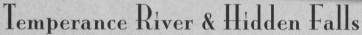

Temperance River & Hidden Falls

A mile up Highway 61 from Cross River the Temperance River, the focal point of Temperance River State Park, plays host to the dangerous beauty of Hidden Falls. A series of cascades brings the river down 162 feet through a rocky gorge within the space of only half a mile. The last cascade drops just one hundred feet from the river's mouth. Along this span, the river's erosive power has carved deep cauldrons into the native rock, thus "hiding" the falls (also called the Temperance River Gorge). Missteps have led to tragedies over the years, as hikers have accidentally dropped into the gorge.

The area surrounding the river became a state park in 1938. The Ojibwe name for the river is *Kawimbashzibi* or "Deep Hollow Water River." The name "Temperance" is actually a play on words: the river's sheer drop allows it to empty into Lake Superior without leaving behind much sediment or vegetation, and therefore the mouth of the Temperance has no "bar."

Tofte & Lutsen

Tofte takes its name from the town of Toftevaage, Norway, the birthplace of brothers John and Andrew Tofte and Hans and Torget Engelson, who took up housing in abandoned homesteads after arriving there on the steamer *Dixon* on May 12, 1893. (They had first named the town "Carlton" for nearby Carlton Peak, but that name was already in use.) The Norwegians logged, farmed, and mostly fished to earn their keep. A forest fire raged through the town in 1910, destroying most of the structures (they were later rebuilt). The town's fishing heritage made it a natural location for the North Shore Commercial Fishing Museum.

It was a Swedish, not Norwegian, immigrant who settled Lutsen, Cook County's third permanent settlement (only Grand Portage and Grand Marais preceded it). Carl Axel "Charlie" Nelson (born in Norkoping, Ostergotland, Sweden, in 1863) came to the United States when he was eighteen, eventually finding work in Duluth on the fishing tug *Evaston*. After toying with the idea of working with Alfred Merritt on the Arrowhead's iron range, he contracted with the A. Booth Company to set up a fishery, which he established near the Poplar River. Today, of course, tourism dominates Lutsen, in no small part due to Nelson himself, who opened the famous Lutsen Resort.

POPLAR RIVER AT LUTSEN, HIGHWAY No. 1, NORTH SHORE, LAKE SUPERIOR   107531

Poplar River

The Poplar River—at whose mouth was found the homestead of Lutsen's founder, Charlie Nelson (see sidebar)—takes its Anglicized name directly from the Ojibwe name, *Gamanazadikizibi* or "Place-of-Poplars River." The Poplar is perhaps best known as the site of Nelson's Lutsen Resort, which he first called "Lutzen House" when he began hosting hunters, anglers, and occasionally those who suffered from hay fever or tuberculosis starting around 1900. Today the area includes the resort's Swedish lodge (designed by Edwin Lundie in 1952), Lutsen Mountain ski hill (opened in 1948), and a golf course layed out along the Poplar's banks.

Grand Marais

The natural harbor found about halfway between the Temperance River and the Canadian border once contained a large marsh, causing French trappers to name the spot Grand Marais, "great marsh." (The Ojibwe named the area *Kitchi-Bitobig* or "double body of water" for the two separate areas formed by the town's twin bays.) The American Fur Company operated a fishing station at Grand Marais as early as 1823, but it was gone by 1840 and no settlement communities were established until the 1854 Treaty of La Pointe opened the North Shore to European settlement. Robert McLean brought a party to the site that same year to prospect for rumored veins of copper, gold, silver, and iron ore, but little materialized. In 1856 John Godfrey (some accounts record his first name as Richard) set up a trading post and has since been considered the town's first permanent resident. But Godfrey became discouraged and returned to his native Detroit just a few years later.

130-D—Airplane View of Beautiful Harbor, Grand Marais, Minn. Minnesota's Scenic North Shore Drive

8A-H2318

IN THE MINNESOTA ARROWHEAD COUNTRY.

"THE BREAKERS" EAST HARBOR, GRAND MARAIS, MINN.

109297

The town didn't see significant growth until the fishing industry picked up and regional logging started in 1871 to feed the growth of Duluth. During the 1870s Henry Mayhew, Samuel Howenstein, and Ted Wakelin settled on the bay, purchased most of the surrounding land, and developed warehouses, docks, and a railroad right-of-way.

No roads reached the outpost, so all goods had to arrive by boat. Henry and Thomas Mayhew opened a store that also served as a trading post. Tourists began arriving as early as 1890, and today Grand Marais remains the North Shore's biggest visitor destination.

158-D—Harbor Entrance, Grand Marais, Minn.

155-D—Entrance to Grand Marais Harbor, Lake Superior

At settler John Godfrey's behest, Congress appropriated $6,000 to build a lighthouse at Grand Marais in 1856—but it never materialized. Thirty years later, as Grand Marais had become a center for logging and fishing, the natural harbor town saw more and more shipping traffic, raising safety concerns. In 1885 Congress made $9,552 available for a lighthouse, and the next year a thirty-two foot pyramid-shaped tower sporting a fifth-order Fresnel lens stood watch over the harbor (pictured in the postcards). It included a 1,500 pound fog bell taken from the Passage Island Lighthouse off Isle Royale in 1884. Joseph Mayhew became the lighthouse's first keeper.

Cascade Lodge, Grand Marais, Minn.

Cascade Lodge

Two of the North Shore's most famous private lodges—Naniboujou and Cascade Lodge—are found on either side of Grand Marais. Cascade is located about nine miles southwest of Grand Marais and just east of the Cascade River on land Edward Ogilvie purchased in 1922. He opened the lodge in 1927, also offering summer housing in three cabins. The first lodge building was torn down just twelve years later to make room for a grander structure (above), which was expanded in 1957. Business took off after the North Shore Road was fully paved in 1933 and a boost was provided by the promotion of the North Shore as "America's Hay Fever Haven." When the Lutsen Ski area opened in 1948, the Lodge stayed open year round.

Naniboujou Club

Five businessmen from Duluth (including R. D. Handy, a postcard publisher) created the Naniboujou Lodge, a private (and quite grand) sportsman's getaway fifteen miles northeast of Grand Marais, which opened in 1927. The lodge takes its name from Nanaboozoo ("trembling tail"), a trickster character of Ojibwe legend, a spirit or a half man/half woman archetype who had many misadventures.

Among its more famous members were boxer Jack Dempsey, Babe Ruth, and writer Ring Lardner. The resort is expansive, boasting a half-mile of shoreline on either side of the mouth of the Brule River (site of Devil's Kettle Falls). When first developed, it encompassed 3,300 acres, much of which is now part of Judge C. R. Magney State Park. It boasted a grand lodge (pictured) and plans were made for tennis courts and other amenities. Unfortunately, the Lodge only drew half of the one thousand members it needed to survive. It was turned over to a hotel chain in the 1930s.

Spirit Little Cedar Tree

The Spirit Little Cedar Tree (*Minido Geezhigans* in Ojibwe; also known disrespectfully as the "Witch Tree" or "Witch's Tree") is a cedar monarch that sprouted from seemingly barren rock on the Hat Point prominence some four hundred years ago. (Erosion actually wore away the soil in which the tree first took seed, and its roots have grown beyond what has been worn away, giving the appearance of a tree growing from rock.) For generations the Ojibwe left offerings of tobacco at the tree for safe passage on the big lake. When they encountered Grand Portage, French voyageurs respected the tradition and left offerings of their own. Reports conflict as to how it came to be called the "Witch Tree." Some say it was given that name by early European explorers; others give credit to Dewey Albinson,

one of many artists drawn to draw the tree (such as Kent Aldrich, who made the woodcut at right).

Unfortunately, vandals have carved their initials in the tree and clipped branches as souvenirs, forcing the local band of Grand Portage Ojibwe, who now own the land near Grand Portage where the tree is found, to close public access to the Spirit Little Cedar Tree.

Grand Portage

The town of Grand Portage, platted on a bay off Hat Point, marks the starting point of a path to the Pigeon River that bypasses a twenty-mile stretch of the waterway containing High Falls and impassable rapids (see next page). Before the voyageurs arrived and gave the site its French name, the Ojibwe used the portage for generations and called it *Gitcheonigaming* or "great carrying place." France's Pierre La Verendrye arrived at Grand Portage in 1731 along with his sons and fifty French soldiers. When the British Northwest Company set up a trading post in the late 1700s, the town became one of the most important fur trading centers in North America. Today Grand Portage sits on land owned by the Grand Portage Band of Ojibwe. Grand Marais' first settler, John Godfrey, named the nearby Mount Josephine—actually an outcrop of rock thought to be some of the oldest in the world, roughly 1.3 billion years old—for his daughter who, along with some friends, climbed the peak in 1853.

PIGEON RIVER FALLS, INTERNATIONAL BOUNDARY, MINNESOTA ARROWHEAD COUNTRY

PIGEON RIVER FALLS AT CANADIAN BORDER — MINNESOTA ARROWHEAD COUNTRY

Pigeon River

Each spring passenger pigeons would arrive near a Lake Superior tributary to breed; the local Ojibwe would use large nets to snare the birds, which they called *Omimi*, and so they named the river *Omimizibi* after the birds. The passenger pigeon went extinct by 1900, but the Pigeon River continues to flow. Outside of the St. Louis River, the Pigeon is the largest river feeding Lake Superior and acts as a border between the United States and Canada (see page 12). Two miles from its mouth, Middle Falls drops the river 70 feet; upstream the highest waterfall in Minnesota, High Falls, cascades 120 feet.

Isle Royale

The largest island on Lake Superior, Isle Royale sits eighteen miles from the Canadian shore and fifty-five miles from Michigan's Upper Peninsula (it is actually part of Michigan, not Minnesota). Stretching forty-five miles long and between three and ten miles across, the 850-square-mile island forms the eye of Lake Superior's wolf-head shape. Many smaller islands surround it. It was first called *Minong* by the Ojibwe, a word that roughly translates to "a good place."

Ancient Native Americans called the Old Copper peoples once populated the island, mining its rich copper beds. They extracted the mineral by heating the native rock with fire and then dousing it with cold water, causing the rock to crumble, leaving the copper behind. They then extracted the larger pieces for use as hammers and chisels, but never developed a method for heating the smaller particles. In the early 1920s Pennsylvania newspaper editor William P. F. Ferguson excavated the purported remains of an Old Copper village near the site of ancient copper mines, but the authenticity of his findings were debated. When European settlers tried to revive

ALONG THE ROCKY SHORE, ISLE ROYALE, LAKE SUPERIOR—6

ISLE ROYALE, LAKE SUPERIOR, NEAR DULUTH

No. 582. V. O. Hammon Pub. Co., Chicago

Isle Royale's Chippewa Harbor, whose terrain is described as "fjord-like." The Army Corps of Engineers actually blasted out some of its rock to make the harbor safer to navigate.

copper mining on the island in the 1840s (the island was then rumored to be made entirely of copper), they found little activity by natives outside of a seasonal fishing site on Grace Island and a maple sugaring camp at Sugar Mountain. Copper enterprises would come and go again in the 1870s and 1890s.

Some of those miners stayed to try their hands at commercial fishing, which first came to the island in 1800 with the Hudson's Bay Company. Later the American Fur Post fishing fleet would thrive on Isle Royale, particularly between 1837

In 1902 Tobin's Harbor fisherman Gus Mattson hauled in his nets for the last time and established a vacation retreat later named Tobin's Harbor Resort. Subsequent owners renamed the resort Minong Lodge, and it acted as the focal point of what was then Isle Royale's largest harbor community. It was closed by the National Park Service who purchased it when the entire island became a park in 1931.

and 1841, when the company employed thirty fishermen and an untold number of Ojibwe and Metis women, who worked cleaning fish. The American Fur Post's operations ceased in 1842, and commercial fishing went dormant until the 1870s, when the region's increased population created a large market.

Light House at Rock Harbor, Lake Superior.

ROCK HARBOR, ISLE ROYALE, LAKE SUPERIOR.

Built in 1856, the Rock Harbor Lighthouse, a rubble-stone tower nearly fifty feet high with a domed copper roof, sports a fourth-order Fresnel lens. It operated for three years before being abandoned by its keeper after mining operations closed and marine traffic declined. It was reopened following a renovation in 1873, but eventually shut down again in 1879 after the Menagerie Island Lighthouse, built in 1875, rendered the Rock Harbor light unnecessary. In the 1930s it was used as a base of operation for a few fisherman and had to be stabilized in the 1950s to prevent it from tipping over.

Many individuals and fisheries operated from the island, but by far the largest was the A. Booth Company, which recruited fishermen from Norway, offering them equipment, housing, and supplies on credit until they had made their money back. By 1915 more than one hundred fishermen worked the waters around Isle Royale.

In 1931 President Herbert Hoover signed a congressional authorization to conserve "a prime example of North Woods Wilderness." Nine years later President Franklin D. Roosevelt established Isle Royale National Park. This act, along with the invasion of exotic fish such as smelt and the sea lamprey, dramatically reduced commercial fishing. As of 1990 only one fisherman dropped his nets near Isle Royale, operating a family fishery over one hundred years old.

Many of Isle Royale's one-time fishermen turned to tourism to earn their keep, some long before the industry died out. John's Hotel, the island's first resort, was built in 1894. Other resorts and lodges soon followed, offering guests such activities as dancing, tennis, bowling, and fishing—they even built a golf course on Belle Isle. Like the North Shore, Isle Royale was promoted as a haven for hay fever sufferers. By the 1930s the archipelago's smaller islands were dotted with summer homes. Today much of Isle Royale, despite its long history of human activity, remains an untamed wilderness.

Washington Harbor, located on the southwestern tip of Isle Royale, is the first impression most visitors have of the island, as it is the destination of excursion boats from Minnesota and Ontario.

The Steamer *America* and other Isle Royale Shipwrecks

The Isle Royale archipelago is made up of many smaller is-lands and dotted with reefs and rocks, making its shipping lanes very dangerous to navigate. At least a dozen ships have wrecked off Isle Royale, including the *Cumberland* (1877), the *Emperor* (1877), the *Algoma* (1885), the *Chisholm* (1898), the *Monarch* (1906), the *Chester A. Congdon* (1918), the *Glenyon* (1924), the *Kamloops* (1927), the *America* (1928), and the *George M. Cox* (1933).

The *America*, owned by the A. Booth Company, was a beloved ship on Lake Superior, serving for most of its life as a transportation link between Duluth, Port Arthur, Isle Royale, and settlements along the North Shore (which also made the *America* an important communication tool). In 1908 a forest fire threatened those very North Shore townships, and Minnesota's governor called on the *America* to evacuate Beaver Bay. She rescued about three hundred villagers. On June 6, 1928, the *America* left Grand Marais for Isle Royale to drop off passengers before heading to Port Arthur. In the early morning hours of June 7, she struck a reef near Isle Royale's Washington Harbor, skidding over the rocks four times and ripping a hole in her hull just be-low the engine room on the starboard side. The ship's pumps couldn't keep up with the water pouring in. The captain or-dered the ship to steer for the north gap of Washington Har-bor in an attempt to beach her, but it struck more rocks and stopped ninety feet from shore. All thirty-one passengers and crew managed to get off the *America* before she slid off into deep water.

11293.   *Steamer America in Washington Harbor, Isle Royle.*

The steamer America *in a postcard view captured before 1915 at* Washington Harbor—*the very port at which she would sink in 1928.*

THE RUGGED SHORE AND LIGHTHOUSE, ISLE ROYALE, LAKE SUPERIOR—3

Located off the northeastern tip of Isle Royale, Passage Island Lighthouse was built in 1881 using $5,000 appropriated by Congress. Blueprints for the structure duplicate those of earlier light stations built elsewhere using the Norman Gothic style. The two-story structure was made of fieldstone and boasts a fourth-order Fresnel lens. In 1882 a 1,500-pound steam-powered fog bell was installed; in 1895 keepers shovelled thirty-five tons of coal that kept the whistle blowing for 755 hours. (The whistle would later be moved to the lighthouse at Grand Marais.) The lighthouse still helps watercraft navigate the lake, but its Fresnel lens was replaced by an acrylic optic lens in 1998.

The Rock of Ages Lighthouse sits on a rock outcropping about two-and-a-half miles from the southwestern tip of Isle Royale. After local authorities spent many frustrating years trying to convince Congress of a need for the light, it was finally built between 1908 and 1909 at a cost of $115,000. It stands eight stories high, providing ample room for the keeper and his assistant, and the entire building was heated by a steam plant located in the structure's upper cellar. Four keepers were assigned to the light, and each received a week of leave each month. In 1933 the George M. Cox rammed a nearby reef in heavy fog, and the keepers saved all 125 passengers and crew members.

ROCK OF AGES LIGHT HOUSE, WASHINGTON HARBOR, ISLE ROYALE NATIONAL PARK

Part II

DULUTH, Minn. From Forest to Mill.

Logging the Arrowhead

Logging the Arrowhead

Much of the logging in the western Lake Superior region took place in the Arrowhead along the lake's North Shore (northern Wisconsin was also logged thoroughly, as were Isle Royale and the Apostle Islands). Minnesota lumberjacks felled enough timber between 1891 and 1924 to produce nearly eight billion board feet of lumber.

The work was hard and the conditions cold; the logging season stretched from November to April as the frozen ground prevented oxen and draft horses from bogging down under their heavy loads. At the work site, the foreman oversaw everything, from the

TYPICAL LUMBER JACKS OF NORTHERN MINNESOTA

Logging Scene near Duluth.

...ber Camp, Northern Minnesota.

building of the camp to tree selection—even where the trees should fall (a timber cruiser or "landlooker" was sent ahead by lumber companies to scout which stands of trees to harvest). A logging crew typically consisted of two sawyers, a swamper, a chainer, a teamster, a sled tender, a decker, and a groundhog.

The sawyers notched trees with an axe then worked in pairs with a cross-cut saw to take the tree down; on a good day a team of sawyers could cut up to one hundred white pines. Swampers trimmed limbs off felled trees, cleared brush, kept roadways clear, and removed manure.

4. DOWNING TIMBER, NORTHERN MINNESOTA.

507—Cutting Timber, Duluth, Minn.

OODSMEN OF NORTHWEST

NO. 37. SKIDDING IN THE NORTHERN WOODS.

5. HAULING RAW MATERIAL, NORTHERN WOODS

Teamsters (also called skidders) used horses to pull felled trees from where they were cut to landing areas where they were later loaded and sent to lumber mills. If the tree was less than a mile from the loading area, it was dragged out with chains (attached by the chainer to a go-devil, a wishbone-shaped tree crotch); when trees were felled further away, the groundhogs stacked logs on sleighs pulled by teams of oxen or draft horses using cant hooks. (Horses were later replaced by steam powered tractors called log-haulers, which could pull several sleighs). The road monkey was the man in charge of building and maintaining logging roads, often made of ice so the sleighs could move more easily. Along downhill grades of the ice roads, a worker called the hayman-on-the-hill threw down hay to slow the sleighs so they would not overcome the teams of horses pulling them.

One site of the North Shore's logging heyday has become a stunning spot to view fall colors. Heartbreak Ridge (located northwest of Schroeder on Forest Road 166, west of the Sawbill Trail) takes its name from its steep grade, which was often too much for even the sturdiest of horses when it was covered

"A Logging Scene."   Duluth, Min.

with ice and snow. Consequently, teamsters could not move logs up and down the rise, and bypassing the ridge created extra work; they spent more time removing fewer trees, thereby making less money, and breaking their hearts.

Once at the landing area, deckers made parallel stacks of logs so they could more easily be rolled into the river for transport to the mills. In the water men tied the logs into giant rafts (pictured on page 69) which they floated or towed downstream to Lake Superior and the mills. The men who worked these rafts—called rivermen, river drivers, and riverhogs—used a cant hook to maneuver logs. Their task was called cordelling: walking along the river bank keeping the logs moving wherever boats could not help navigate the rafts. Occasionally they had to walk out on the logs to keep a raft moving. This job was the task of the birler, a highly skilled river hog who wore calked (spiked) boots and used small, quick steps to spin logs into place as he moved about a log raft. After a successful run

A Logging Scene.   Duluth, Minn.

David N.

Logging the Arrowhead

bringing logs to the mills, birlers would sometimes compete with each other, two on a log, trying to see who could make the other fall off; this activity developed into the sport of logrolling. Occasionally logs would pile up during a drive, creating a literal logjam. In extreme cases, dynamite was used to clear the jams (remnants of jam-clearing blasts can be seen along the Cross River).

Once a raft was brought to Lake Superior's shores, logging outfits leased tugs, steam barges, and scows to tow them to mills in Duluth; Ashland, Wisconsin; Baraga, Michigan; and other mill towns. Later trains were used to transport the logs; flat cars were loaded at first by a loading gang of groundhogs using jammers, crane-like devices powered by horse (they were eventually replaced with steam loaders like those pictured in the postcards on the facing page). Lumber companies laid

LUMBERING NEAR DULUTH, DULUTH, MINN.

hundreds of miles of track to harvest trees on the North Shore. Trucks have been used since the 1930s.

The success of the logging industry rose and fell with the economy—when Duluth boomed, so did timber production. Major logging outfits included the Schroeder Company, which logged along the Cross and Temperance rivers, and the Alger-Smith Company, the largest operation to log the Arrowhead. Logging reached its peak during the first decade of the twentieth century and was thought all but dead in Duluth by 1920. Still, it hung on through the twenties, but was hit particularly hard by the Great Depression and the creation of the Superior National Forest, and never quite recovered. In 1941 the last logging railroad was dismantled.

Some logging still takes place in northern Minnesota, but most of it is done outside the Arrowhead region. Today's loggers use heavy machinery rather than hand tools, and transport logs on flatbed semis. But some things never change: in January 2006, Minnesota logging companies reported that production had been slowed by the unusually warm winter, causing logging trucks—like the teams of oxen and draft horses before them—great difficulty when moving their heavy loads over the soft, unfrozen ground. Heartbreak Ridge all over again.

Steam Log Loader.

LUMBERING, NEAR DULUTH, MINN.

BUNK HOUSE IN LOGGING CAMP IN NOTHERN MINNESOTA.

E. O. HARMON PUB. CO., MINNEAPOLIS & CHICAGO.

View of Lumber Camp near Duluth, Minn.

Lumber Camp Life

Life in a lumber camp was no stack o' flapjacks, although much of it revolved around the cook and his crew, which included a helper called a cookie and a chore boy known as the bull cook. The camp woke at 5 A.M.; breakfast came an hour later. The jacks had twelve minutes to eat, and the cooks allowed no talking (most likely to thwart criticism that could escalate into mutiny; if the crew was dissatisfied with the chow, their recourse was to stop work in protest, an action called "walking the cook"). They then went straight to work until 11:30 A.M., when the bull cook brought them flaggins, hot lunches packed in large cans. At noon they were back to work and toiled until the sun set. After a leisurely twenty-minute dinner, the loggers occupied themselves by relaxing on long pew-like seats called deacon's benches, repairing clothes and equipment or playing a few hands of cards. Lights went out at 9 P.M. Besides the jacks and the cooking crew, the camp was populated by the camp's clerk, called an inkslinger. Most camps were small; a camp of forty to fifty men was considered large.

Logging Crew---"Dinner Out" ne[...]

7 NOONDAY LUNCH, NORTHERN MINNESOTA. 1910

On Sundays the men were allowed to bathe and boil up their clothes (washing them by placing them in boiling water), write letters home, and pack their beds with fresh straw. On days off they would travel to Duluth to spend their money. The Schroeder Company actually built two saloons and a brothel in order to keep men in camp on their days off—too often a trip to Duluth was extended by a stay in the local jail, and missing jacks slowed production. When a camp needed workers, they relied on recruiters to fill the roles; these men were known as man-catchers.

Logging was dangerous work; with men slinging axes, saws, and cants—as well as trees falling and logs rolling—injuries were commonplace (a broken arm or limb was called a cracked stem). Consequently, many loggers ended up in the hospitals of Duluth and Superior. Sister Amata of Duluth's St. Mary's Hospital realized that lumbermen were rarely flush with money, so she sold those who worked the lumber camps a precursor to health insurance called "lumberjack hospital tickets" for seventy cents a month. The cards guaranteed the jacks medical care and a bed. It was one of the first plans of its kind in the nation. Nuns who worked for Superior's St. Francis Hospital sold a similar plan to both lumbermen and dock workers for an annual "donation" of five or ten dollars.

Off to the Mills

Henry W. Wheeler built Duluth's first sawmill in 1856, and within a few years mills dotted the North Shore from the Twin Ports to Beaver Bay. Firms such as Culver & Nettleton, Duncan & Brewer, Alger-Smith Company, Schroeder Company, Scott Graff Lumber, Oneota Lumber Company, Hubbard & Vincent, Mitchell & McClure, Merrill & Ring, Huntress & Brown, Clark & Jackson, and many others operated mills wherever log rafts, and later trains, could reach them.

In the 1880s area mills produced an average of 10 million board feet a year; in 1890 they produced 150 million feet. By 1894 thirty-two mills employed 7,700 workers in Duluth and Superior alone. The peak year for Twin Ports milling was 1902, when 443 million board feet were produced. During the first ten years of the twentieth century over 3 billion board feet of

Logging Train in the North Woods near Duluth.

LUMBERING NEAR DULUTH. (LOGGING TRAIN THAT WALKS ON THE SNOW). DULUTH, MINN.

G-18—Logs Ready for

lumber came out of Duluth's mills, but just over 1 billion feet was cut from 1910 to 1921, the year many declared the industry played out. Indeed, the milling industry had been in decline since at least 1910, when Twin Ports operations dropped to just six major mills; by 1925 only one mill operated out of Duluth.

Once the logs reached the mills, either by rail or water, the raw material was turned into lumber. The logs were placed into a barker, a machine which stripped off the bark. Once stripped, sawyers ran the logs through a variety of saws, starting with the

double gang, a large set of parallel blades powered by water that sawed the logs into boards. Gate saws (sometimes called sash or frame saws), which sat in a frame and moved up and down by power generated from the mill's waterwheel, were also used. (A gang saw was a set of gate saws working in unison.) Ripsaws

Interstate Bridge, Duluth, Minn.

orthern Minnesota

7454. A LUMBER RAFT, DULUTH, MINN.

DETROIT PUBLISHING CO.

Menominee Saturday 1:25 from Escanaba

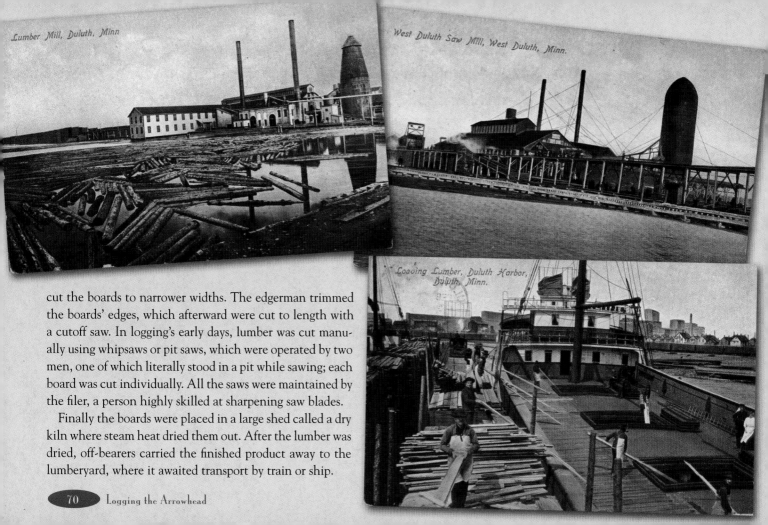

Lumber Mill, Duluth, Minn

West Duluth Saw Mill, West Duluth, Minn.

Loading Lumber, Duluth Harbor, Duluth, Minn.

cut the boards to narrower widths. The edgerman trimmed the boards' edges, which afterward were cut to length with a cutoff saw. In logging's early days, lumber was cut manually using whipsaws or pit saws, which were operated by two men, one of which literally stood in a pit while sawing; each board was cut individually. All the saws were maintained by the filer, a person highly skilled at sharpening saw blades.

Finally the boards were placed in a large shed called a dry kiln where steam heat dried them out. After the lumber was dried, off-bearers carried the finished product away to the lumberyard, where it awaited transport by train or ship.

Part III

HAPPY DAYS ARE HERE

SUPERIOR NATIONAL FOREST IN ARROW HEAD COUNTY, MINN.

Canoe Country

Superior National Forest

Logging activity along Lake Superior's Minnesota north shore between 1870 and 1920 nearly cut the wilderness clean. Some called for portions of the forest to be left untouched, causing lumber companies to threaten to pull out of the region, which at the time would have substantially damaged the local economy by leaving many immigrants unemployed. Christopher Andrews, who had served as a Union general during the Civil War, took up the cause of those who wanted to save part of the forest, organizing what would become Minnesota's state and national forest systems. As a result, in 1909 thirty-six thousand acres were set aside, creating the Superior National Forest. The Forest has since been expanded to include much of the Arrowhead, from the Pigeon River west to Lake Vermilion, and from the Canadian border to stretches of the North Shore.

The Forest contains 3,886 sites of early human habitation, evidence that it has been populated by humans for over ten thousand years. More recent evidence includes pictographs, rock drawings left behind most likely by Ojibwe artists sometime during the past five hundred years (see page 85). French trappers known as voyageurs worked the region as early as the 1700s.

During the Great Depression, the projects in the Forest helped create jobs. In 1936 the *Duluth News-Tribune* reported that fifteen Civilian Conservation Corps camps operated in the Forest, with about two hundred men enrolled in each camp.

Consisting of fir, spruce, aspen, birch, and maple trees, Superior National is the largest forest in the United States outside of Alaska. Trails for hiking, Nordic skiing, biking, horse-back riding, and snowmobiles cover two thousand miles.

The Forest is among the largest nesting spots for bald eagles in the lower forty-eight states, and is also home to an abundance of other wildlife, including loons, osprey, eagles, otters, deer, moose, black bears, Canadian lynx, and the gray wolf. In fact, northern Minnesota has the last population of gray wolves in the lower forty-eight states, with about 350 wolves roaming the Superior National Forest alone—and the International Wolf Center makes its home in the Boundary Waters Canoe Area Wilderness's unofficial western gateway of Ely, Minnesota. And, of course, the Forest is also the home of a certain rodent that brought the French (and, subsequently, the industrialized development of the entire region) to western Lake Superior way back in the seventeenth century: the beaver.

Today the northern one-third of the Superior National Forest also contains the B.W.C.A.W. (see pages 82–85), the largest protected wilderness area in the lower forty-eight states.

A MOOSE FAMILY IN THE SUPERIOR NATIONAL FOREST

SKY BLUE WATERS AND SILVER BIRCHES

Just shy of Ilgen City on Highway 61, Highway 1 twists and turns its way relatively northwest to Ely, passing two tiny Finnish settlements along the way: Finland and Isabella.

Found on the banks of the Baptism River, Finland was settled first at the turn of the last century by Finnish immigrants who (obviously) named it for their homeland. They lived off fish and game as they cleared the land to farm barley, oats, and potatoes, and in 1905 established a school. By 1935 there were 179 Finnish families farming 494 acres of hay and other crops. They lived off the land, with some cream sold as the community's only commercial export. Each March Finland celebrates St. Urho's Day, a Finnish version of St. Patrick's Day developed among the Finns of the Arrowhead region in the 1950s.

Settlers reached Isabella as early as the 1890s, but didn't stick around. The Ahlbeck family, Isabella's first known immigrant settlers, homesteaded in the area in 1906. Other Finns joined them in farming the area, mostly growing root vegetables such as beets, rutabagas, and potatoes. For some time logging operations in the area aided the community's economy. The origins of the name "Isabella" are unclear, but it sure has a more pleasant ring to it than the one it beat out in an election: Hurry Up, Minnesota— a moniker decrying the area's brief growing season.

Sawbill & Caribou Trails

The Sawbill Trail (Cook County Road 2) is a primarily gravel road that roughly follows the Temperance River twenty-three miles from Sawbill Lake at the edge of the B.W.C.A.W. to the town of Tofte on the Lake Superior shore.

In 1924 the people of Tofte (see page 47) passed a $20,000 bond to build roads to Sawbill, Cascade, and Caribou lakes. At the time the township reached from the North Shore to the Canadian border, and the success of the Gunflint Trail had city

NORTHERN MINNESOTA

leaders thinking tourism (and the road constructon itself) would aid the local economy. Since logging companies still worked the area—and paid taxes—raising the money wouldn't be too much of a problem. It took until 1932 for workers to reach Sawbill Lake. Built in part through areas of marshy land, the trail was often impassable during spring thaws. Today the first six miles are paved, then the road transitions to gravel; the last six-mile stretch remains in its original condition.

The Caribou Trail (Cook County Road 4) is much less travelled than the Sawbill. It runs twenty miles from Cascade Lake (about eight miles from the B.W.C.A.W.) to Tofte on the shore, passing Caribou Lake along the way. The stretch between Lutsen and Caribou Lake is paved, but the rest is gravel. It may be a rough ride, but taking the Caribou Trail to its terminus at Forest Road 170 leads to Eagle Mountain. At 2,301 feet above sea level, it's not really a mountain, but trekking there from the Lake Superior shore on the Superior Hiking Trail takes you from Minnesota's lowest point to its highest. Along the trail you'll also find White Sky Rock, named in memory of White Sky, an Ojibwe who lived near Lutsen and worked as a forest ranger.

The Honeymoon Trail connects the Sawbill Trail with the Caribou Trail. Legend has it the trail earned its romantic name after John Mulligan, Superior National Forest's first ranger, walked the trail on the way to the Four Mile Lake Ranger Station (he named nearby Grace Lake for his wife and several other area lakes after his daughters).

The cards on this and the facing page are not of the Sawbill or Caribou Trails, but they are lovely views of trails in the Superior National Forest; we've taken a bit of artistic license and used them as an opportunity to discuss those subjects.

WOODSIDE PATH

S-378

MINNESOTA ARROWHEAD COUNTRY

4A-H1785

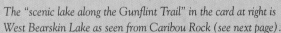

The Pines on Gunflint-Trail

© CURT TEICH & CO. INC.

Minnesota's Superior National Forest

Gunflint & Arrowhead Trails

Angler and outdoor writer Shawn Perich calls the terrain found along the fifty-seven-mile Gunflint Trail "the most spectacular landscape in Minnesota." That's probably not what trader and prospector Henry "Hayes" Mayhew was thinking when he reportedly began removing rocks and trees to clear the trail back in the 1870s—he was searching for silver, as the region was thought to be rich in mineable ores. Mayhew's trail was a wagon road that reached just twenty-four miles to Gunflint Lake (named for the flint found in the rocks that surround it) and eventually reached further north to Rove Lake, where Mayhew set up a trading post in 1875. The trail was called "Mayhew's Road" or "Rove Lake Road." Cook County voted to have the trail extended westward near East Bearskin Lake along an old wagon path beginning in 1891, hoping to aid the local economy by creating infrastucture. By 1893 the trail stretched forty-four miles to just past Gunflint Lake, ready to assist the efforts of the Gun Flint Lake Iron Company, which set up the Paulson Mine.

Scenic Lake along the Gunflint Trail

The "scenic lake along the Gunflint Trail" in the card at right is West Bearskin Lake as seen from Caribou Rock (see next page).

GUNTLINT LAKE, NORTH OF GRAND MARAIS, MINN.

109294

Unfortunately, the Panic of 1893 doomed the enterprise. Since that time the road has been washed out, repaired, rebuilt, re-routed, and constantly improved. Today the entire Gunflint is paved and stretches all the way to Seagull Lake near the Canadian border; only portions of the first twenty-four miles of the modern Gunflint Trail follow Mayhew's path.

The Arrowhead Trail runs from McFarland Lake on the northeastern edge of the B.W.C.A.W. down to Hovland on the Lake Superior shore eighteen miles south. The Trail was originally named the McFarland Road for John McFarland, a settler and mining prospector who arrived in Cook County in 1868 and began building his road in the 1890s when Hovland was still called Chicago Bay; the road was later renamed to promote tourism.

The Gunflint Lodge

By 1930 Cook County boasted thirty resorts, nearly all of them found along the Gunflint Trail. By far the most famous of them all is the Gunflint Lodge. Chicago's Dora Blankenburg and her son Russell opened the Lodge in 1925 (when the Gunflint Trail still only reached a half-mile past Gunflint Lake). A few years later they sold the Lodge to Mae Spunner, whose daughter Justine joined her at the Lodge during the summers. When Mae and Justine opened for their first season in 1929, Justine soon became a jack of all trades, handling everything from accounting to repairing boat motors. She quickly developed friendships with her Ojibwe neighbors, who worked at the resort performing tasks ranging from housekeeping to guiding fishing trips. The Depression forced the Spunners to make the Gunflint their permanent home in 1933. That same year Bill Kerfoot arrived looking for work, and a year later he and Justine married. Justine Kerfoot lived at Gunflint Lodge—in a cabin built in 1935—until she died in 2001.

Hungry Jack

Just south of Bearskin Lake you'll find Hungry Jack Lake, named for Andrew Jackson (Jack) Scott, Sr., a New Jersey native who served as a drummer boy in the Civil War with the Michigan infantry (which marched to the sea with Sherman). After the war he eventually went to New Orleans, working as a hunter to feed lumberjacks logging a cyprus swamp; there he learned to make dugout canoes in the local method. He eventually made it to Duluth by way of Minneapolis and Ashland, Wisconsin, and worked running mail between Superior and Fort William.

He later became a surveyor and guide in Grand Marais. During a surveying expedition in 1873, when stores were dangerously low, Jack's companions snowshoed to Grand Marais for provisions. A blizzard kept them from returning for two weeks, and in the meantime Jack lived off rabbits he trapped, which he thought was stooping beneath his station. When his mates returned and asked, "Are you hungry, Jack?" he replied, "Am I hungry, Jack? I damn near starved to death!" And with this Jack earned his nickname, which was applied to a nearby lake in his honor.

Hungry Jack stayed in Grand Marais to hunt and build his distinctive canoes. Two years after those famished two weeks he married Catherine Boyer, the daughter of a Canadian friend; together they had thirteen children.

West Bearskin Lake

West Bearskin Lake sits roughly twenty-eight miles up the Gunflint Trail. Like most of the lakes along the Gunflint—including East Bearskin and Hungry Jack (see sidebar)—Bearskin is long and narrow in an east/west orientation, as it was carved out of the ground when the glaciers scoured the area during the last ice age.

G-7—A Scenic Northern Lake

8A-H2969

Found just outside the B.W.C.A.W., Bearskin is partially developed, with cabins and cottages nestled in the stands of red and white pine that surround the lake. A great lake for catching trout, its proximity to the Boundary Waters makes it a popular place to launch canoe expeditions, as just one portage takes canoeists into the wilderness.

Bearskin is perhaps best known as the home of Caribou Rock, a fact attested to in the postcards on these pages, all created from images captured from the rock itself. The rock is an outcropping that creates a natural overlook, offering breathtaking views of the lake. Today it is accessed by the Split Pine Trail, which runs for seven miles through the B.W.C.A.W. to Stairway Portage and Stairway Falls (see page 81).

OVERLOOKING BEAR SKIN LAKE FROM CARIBOU ROCK
BACK OF GATEWAY LODGE—44

NATURES BEAUTY
IN THE SUPERIOR NATIONAL FOREST
"IN THE MINNESOTA
ARROWHEAD COUNTRY"—55

Caribou Rock has attracted sightseers since at least the days of the lithographic postcard: the photographs that helped create each one of the cards on this and the facing page were all taken from the rock.

More Lakes Found Near the Gunflint Trail

CLIFF ROCK ON SEA GULL LAKE—46

GOING TO PORTAGE, SEA GULL LAKE—37

MOONLIGHT

BEAUTIFUL GULL LAKE, IN THE HEART OF NORTHERN MINNESOTA

Found at the end of the Gunflint Trail, a portion of Seagull Lake (left and above) lies inside the B.W.C.A.W. The lake's surface covers over four thousand acres and is known for walleye fishing. Motorboats are allowed on the lake but must go no faster than ten m.p.h. Its name derives directly from gayaashk, the Ojibwe name for the American herring gull. The Seagull River connects the lake to Canada's Saganaga Lake (not pictured) further north, and Gull Lake (center of spread) is where the river broadens considerably before flowing into Saganaga—but we can't be sure if the lake in the postcard is that particular Gull Lake. Minnesota has nine lakes named Gull, including four in the Arrowhead: one in St. Louis County, one in Lake County, and two, including the one mentioned above, in Cook County.

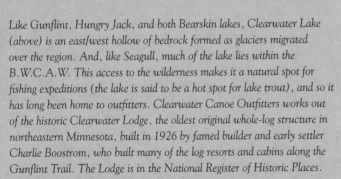

CLEARWATER LAKE, NEAR GRAND MARAIS, MINN.

109235

STAIRWAY FALLS NEAR STAIRWAY PORTAGE

Like Gunflint, Hungry Jack, and both Bearskin lakes, Clearwater Lake (above) is an east/west hollow of bedrock formed as glaciers migrated over the region. And, like Seagull, much of the lake lies within the B.W.C.A.W. This access to the wilderness makes it a natural spot for fishing expeditions (the lake is said to be a hot spot for lake trout), and so it has long been home to outfitters. Clearwater Canoe Outfitters works out of the historic Clearwater Lodge, the oldest original whole-log structure in northeastern Minnesota, built in 1926 by famed builder and early settler Charlie Boostrom, who built many of the log resorts and cabins along the Gunflint Trail. The Lodge is in the National Register of Historic Places.

Stairway Falls (above), located at Stairway Portage at the end of the Caribou Rock Hiking Trail, where Rose Lake drops about thirty feet over the falls and further over some cascades and finally into Duncan Lake. The portage traverses the falls for 138 feet along the creek.

MINNESOTA ARROWHEAD COUNTRY

The B.W.C.A.W.

The Boundary Waters Canoe Area Wilderness takes up roughly the northern one-third of the Superior National Forest. The entire wilderness area contains 1.3 million acres of land, the largest wilderness area in the U.S. east of the Rocky Mountains and north of the Florida Everglades. About 1,175 lakes ranging in size from 10 to 10,000 acres are found within its borders. The surface area of its lakes and streams alone takes up 190,000 acres (roughly 20 percent of the wilderness) providing 1,200 miles of canoe routes, many of which follow the same routes the voyageurs once travelled. Today about two

hundred thousand people visit the B.W.C.A.W. each year, utilizing 2,200 campsites. Motorboats and snowmobiles are allowed (at very limited speeds) to operate on some of the lakes bordering the Wilderness, but for the most part the area has been left in or returned to its natural state.

The land within the B.W.C.A.W. is geologically the lower portion of the Canadian Shield, defined by the Laurentian Divide, a remnant of the ancient Laurentian Mountains (which is why the area is home to the oldest rock in North America). The divide creates two drainage basins in the Wilderness, so its streams and rivers either flow south to Lake Superior or north toward Canada's Hudson Bay (90 percent of the waterways in the B.W.C.A.W. flow north). The Shield is home to four adjoining wilderness areas—the B.W.C.A.W., Voyageur's National Park along the Canadian border near International Falls, and Ontario's Quetico and LaVerendrye provincal parks—creating an ecosystem of more than 2.5 million acres inside 3,859 square miles.

The B.W.C.A.W.'s history is marked with conflict between preservationists and developers. The Superior National Forest was established in 1909, and over the course of the next few decades legislation and battles between the Izaak Walton League (one of the first conservation groups in the U.S., created in Chicago in 1922) and county officials cooperating with resort owners (who in 1923 fought for "a road to every lake") shaped what would become the B.W.C.A.W. The Thye-Blatnik Bill of 1948 (drafted by the Walton League) authorized the government purchase of private holdings within the Wilderness. A year later President Truman banned planes from flying over or landing in the area much to the chagrin of local resort owners, who often flew in sport fisherman. The Wilderness Act of 1964 officially designated the land inside today's B.W.C.A.W. as part of the National Wilderness Preservation System. The Boundary Waters Wilderness Act of 1978 officially named and further protected the area. Battles over such issues as motorboat and snowmobile accesss continue to shape the B.W.C.A.W.

CANOEING ON ONE OF THE THOUSANDS OF LAKES IN THE ARROWHEAD COUNTRY

The Root Beer Lady

Dorothy Molter was the last person to live inside the borders of the B.W.C.A.W. on a permanent basis. In 1930 she moved into an island cabin on Knife Lake, thirty miles north of Ely, and settled in. She made the trip to town for provisions by way of canoe, nordic skis, and snowshoes. In 1952 the *Saturday Evening Post* called her "The Loneliest Woman in America," though that was hardly the case. When the weather allowed, Dorothy enjoyed an almost constant stream of visitors, particularly during the summer months. For a time she operated a small resort and trading post, brewing up homemade root beer for thirsty canoeists, earning her the nickname "The Root Beer Lady" (to cool the drinks in the summer, Molter used lake ice she had packed in moss each spring before the thaw). In 1983 alone, more than 6,500 canoeists signed her guestbook. When a federal law banning permanent residents in the B.W.C.A.W. went into place in 1974, Molter and Benny Ambrose (who lived on Ottertrack Lake) were allowed to stay as "voluntary employees" of the Forest Service (Ambrose died in 1982). Molter lived alone, claiming she never married because "I hate to cook." She died December 18, 1986. Her cabins were later dismantled, moved to Ely, and reconstructed; they are now the main attraction of the town's Dorothy Molter Museum.

Fishing in the B.W.C.A.W.

Of the over two hundred thousand people who visit the B.W.C.A.W. every year to canoe and camp among its waterways, most of them spend time fishing, a fact the postcards on this page attest to. The Wilderness's lakes and streams contain a variety of fish, including many species of pan fish, but most anglers come for the smallmouth bass, lake trout, northern pike, and the tasty walleye, Minnesota's state fish.

Many angling experts argue that the lakes near Ely provide the best smallmouth bass fishing in the world, and lake trout are in abundance throughout the Wilderness because they prefer deep, cold lakes with boulder-strewn bottoms, exactly the kind of lakes left behind by glaciers that scoured the Wilderness ten thousand years ago.

Anglers have set state records for fish pulled out of the Wilderness's lakes. One landed a nearly forty-six pound northern pike from the waters of Lake County's Basswood Lake back in 1929. In 1979 a walleye measuring nearly three feet long and weighing over seventeen pounds was pulled from the Seagull River in Cook County.

"THIS IS THE LIFE"

SUPERIOR NATIONAL FOREST IN ARROW HEAD COUNTY, MINN.

"COME! GAMEY BEAUTIES WAITING HERE"

Minnesota Arrowhead Country

A RECORD CATCH

CATCHES LIKE THESE ARE COMMON IN

Pictographs: Sacred Graffiti or Primitive Postcards?

Among the natural beauty of the B.W.C.A.W. you can find some man-made art: pictographs, images of animals and Ojibwe manitous (spirits) drawn on granite rock faces rising out of the lakes. While theories conflict, most scholars believe most of the pictographs found in the Wilderness were executed by Ojibwe artists, making them no more than a few hundred years old. Many of the drawings represent manitous of the *Midewewin*, a religion practiced by the Ojibwe, such as *Missepishu*, the Great Lynx and master of the underworld. Some may be interpretations of dreams, also important in the *Midewewin* religion. But since similar pictographs have been found further north than the Ojibwe ever reached, more than one culture may have been responsible for them. Some of the images may also be signposts similar to the inuksuit, Inuit rock formations or "men of stone who point the way" left behind for travelers. So perhaps a pictograph such as the one on this page, found on North Hegman Lake, says simply "saw a really big moose here," with the postcard-like implication "wish you were here."

"EVIDENCE OF GOOD LUCK"

"AH! THIS IS THE LIFE"

"A GOOD DAY'S CATCH"

"A DOUBLE LANDING"

"A FINE MESS OF 13 BASS"

Minnesota Arrowhead Country

FISHERMAN'S PARADISE   NORTHERN MINNESOTA

NNESOTA

ENCHANTING BEAUTY
ON WHITE IRON LAKE,
NEAR ELY, MINN.—108

White Iron Lake

White Iron Lake

Located just outside the B.W.C.A.W. a few miles roughly southeast of Ely, White Iron Lake covers 3,429 acres of surface area and is well known for its abundance of northern pike, walleyes, and crappies.

The area was surveyed for a township in 1884, long before any settlers arrived. The likelihood of a community developing looked bleak, as the surveyor described the area as "about as worthless a tract as it is possible to find" and went on to mention rocky, barren soil unfit for agricultural activity and pine trees of limited quality for harvesting. But that didn't stop nine immigrant families from Finland from homesteading the area fifteen years later, when they cleared the land by hand, built log dwellings (and saunas), and sustained themselves by turning the rocky soil into gardens, creating the township of White Iron. By 1920, with the local economy supported in part by a small lumber company, 182 people called the area home.

of Old Indian Portage from White Iron Lake

SILVER RAPIDS, NEAR ELY, MINN.—102

Chief John Beargrease (not the famous North Shore sled dog mail carrier, but perhaps a relative) and his family lived on one of White Iron Lake's islands, referred to as "Indian Island" by local settlers. The Beargreases traded with their Finnish neighbors and two of the chief's daughters married White Iron homesteaders.

The population declined steadily during the Great Depression and never recovered, as many moved to find work after finishing high school. The school the community started in 1903 with seventy-two students closed in 1941.

White Iron Lake is part of a chain that also includes Farm Lake and Garden Lake. Silver Rapids (above) is on the White Iron-Kawishiwi waterway, the site where the White Iron narrows as it flows into the other two lakes. The waterway drains the run-off from the largest watershed in northern Minnesota. Cyrille Fortier, Sr. first built a bridge over the rapids in 1908—just two planks, each wide enough for one horse—as a convenience for settlers and his lumber operation on Garden Lake. In 1930 the township purchased a pre-built metal bridge to traverse the rapids, but it was too short. The river banks had to be filled in to make it fit, which in turn caused flooding each spring. That bridge was replaced in 1972.

Shagawa Lake

Found just north of Ely, Shagawa Lake (once called Long Lake) has long been a center of commercial activity surrounding the tourism trade. Hotels, resorts, and fishing camps have supported the community's economy since at least 1910, and many were found on Shagawa and nearby Burntside Lake (see page 90). Seaplanes such as those pictured below launched from Shagawa to reach resorts deeper into the Superior National Forest along the Canadian border on lakes such as Crooked, Knife, and Basswood. By 1948, twenty-five planes operated out of Shagawa, making it the largest inland seaplane base in the world at the time. But pilots, outfitters, and resort owners who profited from the fly-ins found themselves arguing with local sportsmen who saw their favorite spots depleted of stock; conservationists like Sigurd F. Olson (see page 90) lamented the loss of solitude and silence. Controversy rapidly grew around a movement to ban planes from flying below four thousand feet. Things got ugly. Signatures were forged, lives were threatened, a bomb was thrown. But conservationists prevailed, and in 1949 President Truman signed legislation banning planes from flying low over the area—the first such ban in the world. Some pilots disregarded the law and were later arrested and fined by a federal court.

Seaplane Base on Shagawa Lake, Ely, Minn.

Tourist Camp, Shagawa Lake   Ely, Minn.

SANDY POINT PAR

Summer Day at Sandy Point, Ely, Minn.

ECHO TRAIL, ELY, MINN.—105

Ely's Sandy Point Park on Shagawa Lake was the site of canoe races as early as 1892; watched by thousands, these races were usually won by local Ojibwe. In the winter, ice skating was popular.

Echo Trail

A former logging road, the Echo Trail (St. Louis County Road 166) runs seventy-two miles northwest from Ely to Echo Lake, allowing access to the B.W.C.A.W.'s western lakes. Described as a "rollercoaster ride on asphalt and gravel," the trail developed from the old Ely-Buyck Trail that reached the town of Buyck. It was originally just twelve feet wide, and much of it was built on solid rock, so it drained well and was rarely impassable.

Burntside Lake

BURNTSIDE LAKE, NORTHERN MINNESOTA   4A-H225

Burntside Lake northeast of Shagawa Lake was named by local Ojibwe, who lived on its shores at least thirty years before European settlers arrived. They called it *Ganuboneabikedeagumagsaganing* or "the lake where the timber has been burned off on one side" because a forest fire had once ravaged its north shore. The land surrounding the lake was logged by the St. Croix Lumber Company in 1909. A year later P. T. Brownell and other Ely businessmen bought some of the logged-out property and formed the Burntside Outing Company. They hired Finnish log builders Meitunen and Peterson in 1914 to construct the ten-thousand-square-foot Burntside Lodge; the building is now in the National Register of Historic Places.

Sigurd F. Olson & Listening Point

Arguably Ely's most famous resident, naturalist and writer Sigurd F. Olson (along with his wife, Elizabeth) often retreated to Listening Point, his shoreline property on Burntside Lake. Although Olson had been visiting the area since 1921, he first moved to Ely in 1923 to teach science at Ely Junior College (now Vermilion Community College; in 1936 he would become the college's dean). He spent his summers working as a guide in the region that would become the B.W.C.A.W. after passage of the Wilderness Act of 1964, which Olson had helped to write. Over the years he served as a wilderness ecologist for the Izaak Walton League of America, as vice-president and then president of the National Parks Association, as vice-president and then president of the Wilderness Society, and as an advisor to the National Park Service. His books and essays on natural history and ecology won him the 1974 John Burroughs Medal, nature writing's highest honor. Olsen died in 1982 of a heart attack suffered while snowshoeing; he was eighty-two years old. In 1988 the Listening Point Foundation was established, dedicated to furthering Sigurd Olson's legacy of wilderness education and preserving Listening Point.

A Brief History of Ely

The village of Florence incorporated in 1888 near the east edge of Shagawa Lake on a site now known as Spaulding. Florence, named for the daughter of the Chandler mine's Captain Jack Pengilly (the town's first mayor), was set up as a mining town after the D&IR laid tracks to the area from Tower and opened the Chandler Mine (see page 98). But the community moved after more ore was discovered farther west, and it changed its name as well. "Florence" was already taken, so "Ely" was chosen in honor of mining executive Samuel B. Ely, a big promoter of Vermilion Range ore who lived in Michigan and never actually visited the town that bears his name.

In its first year 177 people lived in the town; seven years later 2,260 residents called Ely home. Many of those drawn to work the area were European immigrants from Norway, Sweden, Finland, Wales, Denmark, Croatia, Slovenia, Austria, and Italy. Language barriers caused these groups to keep to their own, establishing neighborhoods drawn along ethnic lines such as Finn Hill, a hillside community near Shagawa Lake.

Mining helped the town grow, but underground mines needed timber to support shafts, railways that carried the ore needed railroad ties, and lumber was needed to build the miners' homes.

Birds Eye View, Ely, Minn.

GREETINGS FROM ELY MINNESOTA

E-15

© CURT TEICH & CO., INC.

GREETINGS FROM ELY, MINN.

46951

GREETINGS FROM ELY, MINN.

43371

This brought the logging industry to the area, with two large mill operations set up by the St. Croix and Swallow-Hopkins companies east of Ely in Winton. Logging outfits also set up camp on nearby White Iron and Birch lakes.

Meanwhile, the mining company opened other mines in Ely: The Pioneer (1889), the Zenith (1892), the Savoy (1899), and the Sibley (1899). The Pioneer was by far the most productive, producing 41 million tons or 40 percent of the Vermilion Range's entire output. Eventually eleven mines would open near Ely.

Tourism also played a large role in the town's economy, primarily with locals outfitting and guiding visitors on canoe trips and fishing expeditions through the wilderness that surrounds Ely. The Burntside Outing Company opened the Burntside Lodge in 1910 (see page 90). Like Grand Marais (and the Gunflint Trail) in the northeast, today Ely (and the Echo Trail) is considered the western gateway to the B.W.C.A.W.

Today all eleven mines that operated in the Ely area are closed; the Pioneer was the last to operate, closing in 1967. Logging continues in the region, though on a limited scale and only for paper pulp—the major operations virtually disappeared by 1920, when the area's tree reserves were depleted. Tourism, however, continues to fuel the local economy.

CITY HALL, ELY, MINN.—110

COR. SHERIDAN ST.
AND 4TH AVE.
ELY, MINN.

City Hall

Ely's City Hall is actually a multipurpose building, housing not only the city government but also the town's Police and Fire departments—and, one day a month, it acts as the district court as well. Built between 1929 and 1930 at 209 East Chapman Street, the Art Deco structure cost $150,000. When it was dedicated in 1930, Mayor Ernest W. Hanson presided over the laying of the cornerstone—and actually applied the mortar to hold it in place—while more than one thousand people watched (Hanson was a railroad agent who also served as the president of Ely's Chamber of Commerce for many years). Three other buildings proceded it as the town's seat of government, and the building serves the Ely community to this day.

A monument stands on the building's front lawn, dedicated to the memory of the 52 men from the Ely area who died fighting in World War II. Ely had sent 1,600 men to Europe and the Pacific, the largest per-capita enlistment of any city in the U.S. during the war.

The postcard at left is of an unknown residence on Sheridan Street and Fourth Avenue, captured sometime between 1900 and 1915.

Ely High School

High School, Ely, Minn.

Constructed in 1905 of bricks made on site, Ely High School was not the town's first high school; that honor went to the Pioneer School (see sidebar). Ely High served the town until the Memorial School opened in 1924.

Two years before Memorial School opened, Ely Junior College was established with J. H. Santo as dean. The college's twelve students used classrooms at the old High School, sharing it with grade school students. The Junior College moved into Memorial High School when it was built in 1924 and stayed there until 1936. Enrollment jumped during the Great Depression, from 60 students in 1930 to 150 just two years later, as tuition was free and the college charged no lab fees.

After Mr. Santo's death in 1935, noted author and conservationist Sigurd F. Olson (see page 90) became the college's dean, serving at that post until 1946. During Olson's watch, the junior college once again occupied the old High School, utilizing the top two floors while grade school was taught on the lower two floors. The junior college moved to the new Kennedy school in 1959. During the 1960s the college went through several name changes, and by 1971 it was known as Vermilion Community College and had opened its present facility on Camp Street. The Old High School was demolished in 1961.

Other Ely Schools

Ely built Central School—on the site at which the community center now stands—for $630 in 1889. The Ely Public School was erected in 1895 at the corner of Harvey Street and Second Avenue. In 1899 the Pioneer School opened; it was used in part as the high school until the actual high school was built in 1905. It closed in 1941. Washington Grade School was built in 1915 and became a junior high in 1959 when Kennedy School was built to serve elementary and junior college students; today Washington is once again a grade school. In 1921 Ely opened an Industrial Arts Building to teach everything from woodworking to auto repair.

Memorial High School

Construction on Ely's Memorial High School started in July 1923 and finished in September 1924 at a cost of $1 million. In October of that year, the building was dedicated to the memory of the servicemen in the area who fought and died in World War I. The facilities were impressive for their day, including a kiln for pottery, science labratories, a gymnasium with seating for 1,200, and even a natatorium (indoor swimming pool). Two years later it graduated its first class, which consisted of fifty-seven students. For a time Memorial High School was also the home of Ely Junior College (see facing page). Today the school serves as both a junior and senior high school.

Lincoln School, Ely, Minn.

Memorial School Ely, Minn.

Lincoln School

Constructed in 1908 along Second Avenue West between Conan and Harvey streets at a cost of $41,600, Ely's ten-room Lincoln School was built to facilitate a regional population boom during the early 1900s. Before Lincoln opened, the need for classrooms was so great that a store building at the corner of Second Avenue East and Sheridan Street was temporarily turned in to Sletton School. (The building became home to the Martinetto Drug Store.) The school closed at the end of the 1975–1976 school year, and in 1981 it was dismantled.

Shipman Hospital, Ely, Minn.

Presbyterian Church

The Ely Presbyterian Church was first established in 1888—the same year the township itself took root. Only eight souls made up its entire congregation, and they worshipped at Ely's first school "whenever a pastor could be found to conduct the service." The group was officially incorporated just a year later, and by 1890 they had found a pastor in the Reverend T. A. Ambler. They then built themselves a church at 226 East Harvey Street, the first in town. In 1924 that building was replaced by the one featured in the postcard below. In 2002 the church installed new stained-glass windows designed by artist David Hetland.

Shipman Hospital

Ely's first hospital, the Shipman Hospital was built in 1893 by Dr. Charles Shipman, who first arrived in 1888 by train and had to walk the last five miles into town carrying his medical kit. He constructed the hospital (designed by his father, who also designed Wisconsin's original state capitol in Madison) on the corner of Third Avenue and Chapman Street for $7,000, and the local papers announced it by saying Dr. Shipman would "be able to saw off your leg with neatness at an early date." The building served as the Ely Clinic before being demolished after the Ely-Winton Hospital added a clinic building in 1956.

Forest Hotel

The Ely Hotel Association began planning the Forest Hotel as early as 1925 and approved plans that year for the $250,000 hotel. But the hotel wasn't built until 1927 and held its grand opening on January 28, 1928, complete with a banquet and dancing. Helmer Olson won $10 for coming up with the name "Forest Hotel." At one time the hotel contained Vertin's Restaurant and the Buffalo Candy Shop. The building, at 102 West Sheridan Street, was destroyed by fire in 1967. The site became a Bridgeman's, then United National Agency and Queen City Federal Bank.

BURLEY'S FURNISHED LOG CABINS. ELY. MINN.

42570

Burley's Cabins

William and Bessy Burley built Burley's Cabins in 1923 on the southwest shore of White Iron Lake (see page 86). It was one of the earliest resorts in the region, perhaps second only to the Burntside Lodge (see page 90). Ironically, the Great Depression was Burley's boom period, and eighteen log cabins were built at the resort by the time World War II began. The cabins were simply furnished, and the resort offered housekeeping as well as boats and motors for fishing. The Burley's grandson Glenn ran the Restort until it closed in 1975. Today the land it stood on is owned by a private family. All but one of the cabins are gone, but it is being restored and in 2006 its roof and several rotting logs were replaced.

The Vermilion Iron Range

MINING SHAFT, VERMILION IRON RANGE, NEAR ELY

Up until the mid 1850s, the Ojibwe enjoyed being pretty much the only people to populate the lands surrounding what would become Ely; European contact had been limited to French and English fur-trappers, with whom they traded. But a geological survey in 1865 changed all that—it claimed the shores of Lake Vermilion were rich in gold deposits. The following year a gold rush was on. Prospectors found little gold, but blacksmith North Albert Posey found something interesting: a chunk of iron ore. He showed it to Lewis Merritt, who brought it home to his seven sons, telling them the land held iron deposits "worth all the gold in California." But the Merritt brothers didn't seize on their father's idea until 1890 when they opened the Mesabi Iron Range southwest of Lake Vermilion.

In the intervening years eastern capitalist Charlamagne Tower had beaten them to the Vermilion range. In the early 1880s he and his friends opened the Vermilion Iron Range when they created the Minnesota Iron Company and the Duluth & Iron Range Railroad after discovering an extremely high grade iron ore in 1883 near the western edge of today's Miner's Lake. The rich and plentiful iron ore deposits mined by Tower's company were found along the Laurentian Divide, remnants of an ancient chain of mountains called the Vermilion Range. The locomotive Three Spot (see page 26) hauled the first shipment of Vermilion ore from Tower to Agate Bay on July 31, 1884.

The first Vermilion Range mine to operate out of what would become Ely was the Chandler Mine, which shipped its first cargo of ore in 1888. At one point 1,200 men worked the local mines. The Pioneer Mine, the last of eleven mines that operated in the Ely area, closed in 1967. A much more detailed account of the history of the entire Minnesota Iron Range, including its cities and towns and how the mines operated (and lots of historic postcards), will appear in *Greetings from the Arrowhead, Volume 2: The Iron Range*, forthcoming.

Topic Index

References

Books, Articles, and Web sites

Alanen, Arnold R. *A Field Guide to the Architecture and Landscapes of Northeastern Minnesota*. Madison, Wisc.: Department of Landscape Architecture, University of Wisconsin, 2000.

American Life Histories: Manuscripts from the Federal Writer's Project, 1936-1940. "Interview with Dell Chase of Cornell Wisconsin, lumberjack." http://memory.loc.gov/ammem/wpaintro/wpahome.html (accessed November 4, 2006).

Bacig, Tom and Fred Thompson. *Tall Timber: a Pictorial History of Logging in the Upper Midwest*. Bloomington, Minn: Voyageur Press, 1981.

Beymer, Robert. *Superior National Forest: A Complete Recreation Guide for Paddlers, Hikers, Anglers, Campers, Mountain Bikers, And Skiers*. Seattle, Wash.: The Mountaineers, 1989.

Bentley, E. J. *History of Silver Bay Area*. Silver Bay, Minn.: E.J. Bentley, date unknown.

Bell, Mary T. *Cutting Across Time: Logging, Rafting and Milling the Forests of Lake Superior*. Schroeder, Minn: Schroeder Area Historical Society, 1999.

Bishop, Hugh. *By Water and Rail: A History of Lake County, Minnesota*. Duluth, Minn.: Lake Superior Port Cities, 2000.

Centennial Roaring Stoney Days: Ely 1888-1958. Ely, Minn.: Ely-Winton Historical Society, 1958.

Davis, Jessie. *Beaver Bay: Original North Shore Village*. Duluth, Minn: St. Louis County Historical Society; Bay Area Historical Society, 1968.

Dewdney, Selwyn H. *Indian Rock Paintings of the Great Lakes*. Toronto, Canada: University of Toronto, 1962.

Dierckins, Tony. *Zenith: A Postcard Perspective of Historic Duluth*. Duluth, Minn.: X-communication, 2005.

"Ely Historic Building File." Ely, Minn.: Ely-Winton Historical Society, 2004.

Ely, Since 1888: A Piece of Land with the Peace of Water. Ely, Minn.: Ely Echo, 1988.

Furtman, Michael. *Magic on the Rocks: Canoe Country Pictographs*. Duluth, Minn: Birch Portage Press, 2000.

Gale, Thomas P. *Isle Royale: A Photographic History*. Houghton, Mich.: Isle Royale Natural History Association, 1995.

Gilman, Carolyn. *The Grand Portage Story*. St. Paul, Minn.: Minnesota Historical Society Press, 1992.

Glader, Eugene A. *Cascade Lodge: The History of a North Shore Landmark*. Lutsen, Minn.: Cascade Lodge, 2005.

"Great Lakes Vessel Online Index." *Historical Collections of the Great Lakes*. http://digin.bgsu.edu/vsl_sch.htm (accessed November 6, 2006).

Hansen, Mary Alice. *Sawbill: History and Tales*: Tofte, Minn.: Sawbill Press, 2005.

Humphrey, M. J. *Pioneer Faces and Places: Cook County, North Shore, Lake Superior*. Grand Marais, Minn.: Cook County Historical Society, 1979.

Johnston, Basil. *The Manitous: the Spiritual World of the Ojibwes*. New York: HarperCollins, 1995.

Leopard, John. *Duluth, Missabe & Iron Range Railway*. St. Paul, Minn.: MBI Publishing, 2005.

Minahan, Dan. *Memoirs of Knife River*. Knife River, Minn: self published by the author, date unknown.

"Minnesota Travel: Hiking & Waterfalls-Lake Superior Circle Tour." *Superior Trails Web site*. http://www.superiortrails.com/lakesuperior2.html (accessed November 6, 2006).

Ojakangas, Richard W. *Minnesota's Geology*. Minneapolis, Minn.: University of Minnesota Press, 1982.

Olsenius, Richard. *Minnesota Travel Companion: A Guide to History Along Minnesota's Highways*. Minneapolis, Minn.: University of Minnesota Press, 2001.

Pardee, Jack Stone. *The Naniboujou Club*. Naniboujou Lodge, Grand Marais, Minnesota, 1927.

Penner, Myrtle E. *The Hub of the Forest*. Two Harbors, Minn.: self published by the author, 1971.

Pepper, Terry. "Grand Marais Light." *Seeing the Light Web site*. http://www.terrypepper.com/Lights/superior/gdmarais-mn/index.htm (accessed November 6, 2006).

Perich, Shawn. *The North Shore: a Four Season Guide to Minnesota's Favorite Destination*. Duluth, Minn.: Pfeifer-Hamilton, 1992.

Pratt, John. *A Survey of Encampment Forest, Lake County, Minnesota*. Two Harbors, Minn.: self published by the author, 1964.

Raff, Willis. *Pioneers in the Wilderness: Minnesota's Cook County, Grand Marais and the Gunflint in the Nineteenth century*. Grand Marais, Minn.: Cook County Historical Society, 1981.

Sansome, Constance J. *Minnesota Underfoot: A Field Guide to the State's Outstanding Geologic Features*. Bloomington, Minn.: Voyageur Press, 1983.

Schiller, Judi and Richard Schiller "Lake Superior's Wild North Shore" *Crooked Creek Observer Web site*. http://www.emily.net/~schiller/nshore.html (accessed November 4, 2006).

Schwartz, George M.. *Minnesota's Rocks And Waters: A Geological Story*. Minneapolis, Minn.: University of Minnesota Press, 1963.

"Sigurd Olson." *The Listening Point Foundation Web site*. http://www.listeningpointfoundation.org/sigurd.html (accessed November 11, 2006).

Silver Bay History. Silver Bay, Minn.: League of Women Voters, date unknown.

Starkman-Porthan, Mary Ann. *White Iron and Birch Lake, 1898-1920*. Gilbert, Minn.: Self published by the author, 2002.

Stenlund, Milt. *Burntside Lake–the Early Days, 1880-1920*. Ely, Minn.: Ely-Winton Historical Society, 1986.

"State Record Fish." http://www.dnr.state.mn.us/fishing/staterecords.html (accessed November 11, 2006).

Two Harbors in 1910: Lake County, Minnesota. Two Harbors, Minn.: 1910.

Two Harbors, Minn. in 1900. Two Harbors, Minn.: H. Burwell, 1900.

Two Harbors, 100 Years: a Pictorial History of Two Harbors, Minnesota and Surrounding Communities. Two Harbors, Minn.: Lake County Historical Society, 1983.

Van Brunt, Walter, 1846-1928. *Duluth and St. Louis County Minnesota: Their Story and People*. Chicago, Ill.: American Historical Society, 1921.

Writers' Program of the Work Projects Administration in the State of Minnesota. *The WPA Guide to the Minnesota Arrowhead Country*. St. Paul, Minn.: Minnesota Historical Society, 1988.

Newspapers

Duluth Herald

Duluth News-Tribune

Ely Echo

Ely Miner

Image Credits

Lithographic Postcards

The postcard images presented in this book come from cards collected by Herb Dillon, Brad E. Nelson, Jerry Paulson, Jerry Pepper, Bob Swanfeld, the Ely-Winton Historical Society, and the author. The cards were originally published between 1898 and roughly 1950 by a wide variety of publishers who are no longer in business and who left no record of the photographers who captured the original images.

Non-Postcard Images

Map of Minnesota's Arrowhead and Western Lake Superior (page iv) by the author.

Lac Tracy 1671 (page 2); map by an anonymous Jesuit cartographer (most likely Father Claude Jean Allouez or someone traveling with him); courtesy of the Illinois State Museum; tinted by the author.

The *Medeira* (page 37); photograph courtesy of the Lake Superior Maritime Collection; sepia tinted by the author.

John Beargrease (page 38); photograph courtesy of the Lake County Historical Society.

Naniboujou Club (page 50); black & white postcard courtesy Maryanne Norton; sepia tinted by the author.

Spirit Little Cedar Tree (page 51); color woodcut courtesy of Kent Aldrich of the Nomadic Press, St. Paul, Minnesota.

Gunflint Lodge in 1930 (page 77); pastel-tinted photo courtesy of Lee Kerfoot of the Gunflint Lodge.

Pictograph of Moose (page 85); from a public domain photograph of an image made by unknown person, most likely of Ojibwe descent; computer enhanced by the author.

Greetings from the Zenith City!

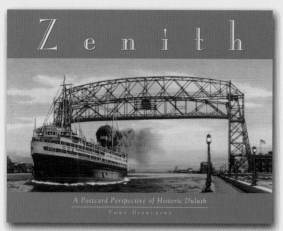

Greetings from Duluth Volumes 1 & 2
Both volumes contain twenty removable reproductions of vintage postcards selected from *Zenith*: Duluth's Aerial Bridge, buildings, parks, waterfront scenes, and more.

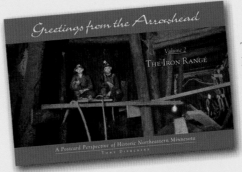

Zenith: A Postcard Perspective of Historic Duluth
Written by Tony Dierckins (*Greetings from the Arrowhead*) and featuring 475 vintage lithographic postcards, *Zenith* is the first full-color history of Duluth and the western Lake Superior region ever published (includes 20 paintings and etchings from the 19th and early 20th centuries). Twice the size of *Greetings from the Arrowhead*, *Zenith* is also available in a stunning limited-run, slip-cased hard-cover edition.

*Greetings from the Arrowhead
Volume 2: The Iron Range*
The history of Minnesota's Iron Range as told through more than 200 vintage postcards, including the mining operations and the towns created around them: Hibbing, Virginia, Eveleth, Ely, Aurora, Hoyt Lakes, Grand Rapids, and many more—including Lake Vermilion, where it all began in the 1880s.

Our archive contains over 1,400 vintage color images of Duluth, the Arrowhead, and Western Lake Superior

Discover more at www.x-communication.org